AS I
REMEMBER

AS I REMEMBER

Ten Scottish Authors Recall
How Writing Began for Them

Edited by Maurice Lindsay

CONTRIBUTORS

George Mackay Brown
George Bruce
Robert Garioch
Maurice Lindsay
Norman MacCaig
Alexander Scott
Iain Crichton Smith
Derick Thomson
Sydney Tremayne
Fred Urquhart

ROBERT HALE LIMITED

ISBN 0 7091 7321

Robert Hale Limited
Clerkenwell House
Clerkenwell Green
London, EC1R 0HT

Photoset by Specialised Offset Services Limited
Printed in Great Britain by
Lowe & Brydone Ltd., Thetford, Norfolk

Contents

Introduction

When I was writing the final chapter of my *History of Scottish Literature**, it occurred to me that very little material was available relating the early experiences of several of the contemporary Scottish writers whose work I most admired to the development of their mature styles. It therefore seemed a good idea to invite some of these poets and novelists, roughly speaking my contemporaries, more or less involved in what Eric Linklater called the "second wind" phase of the Scottish Renaissance, to set down their recollections on how for them writing began. With one exception all those asked to contribute agreed to do so, although as readers will in due course discover, one switch of poets had perforce to be undertaken.

There are various ways in which this anthology may be useful. For admirers of particular writers, now and in the future, it provides personal evidence of unimpeachable veracity. For readers and critics able to assess completed achievement without the distraction of the immediate rivalries and dogmatic prejudices that make contemporary judgement partial and erratic, these autobiographical essays reveal

*Robert Hale, London, 1977

much not only about a number of very different personalities, but much also about the varied influences of the topographical, social and economic differences prevailing in Scotland around the mid-twentieth century. Here are gathered images and impressions of city life from Glasgow, Edinburgh and Aberdeen; from the self-reliant North East, with its ancient involvement in the ways of those who fish the seas; from the Gaelic communities of the North West and the Hebrides, where the oldest of Scotland's three languages survive and, perhaps surprisingly, since it is under siege, flourish in poetry of distinction; and from Scandinavian Orkney, across which the long and fertile shadows of saga and mythology still slant.

First and foremost, however, this book is meant to be immediately enjoyable, enjoyment in the widest sense of the term being the main business of literature. For me, it has been an immense pleasure to gather together so many of my friends into such a diverting and eloquent company.

MAURICE LINDSAY

Milton Hill
Dumbarton
1978

1. An Autobiographical Essay

by George Mackay Brown

Born 1921 in Stromness, Orkney, George Mackay Brown was educated there and at Newbattle Abbey College (Edwin Muir, warden) and Edinburgh University where he read English. He still lives and writes in Stromness. He is unmarried.

The first five years, it's said, is the important time in every life; the basic pattern is set then; what follows, into maturity and white hairs, consists of variations and elaborations of the pattern, repeated over and over. If there are ghosts, it is that somehow the unique pattern must still be there after the death of the body. Every man and woman, however seemingly ordinary and unimportant, has by the mere fact of living set the whole web of human existence trembling, and has changed (however minutely) the history of the race. It is those 'boring' people who are the heroes of modern literature – Prufrock, Leopold Bloom, the ineffectual perfumed shadows that move through Tchekhov's plays and stories, Beckett's tramps.

If the early years are vital to the development of every person's life, they are especially so to a writer. The recollection of his childhood haunted Wordsworth for the rest of his life. The chapter, *Wyre*, in Edwin Muir's *An*

Autobiography, is all-important for readers who have difficulty with his poetry: all the keys and clues are there, in the early years. The rest of *An Autobiography* is thin stuff in comparison, though always deeply interesting.

We are said to experience the whole history of the human race in our brief womb-time;

"We wawl and cry that we are come
To this great stage of fools" ...

We arrive on the scene with a vast heritage of experience: the hunt, the battle, the voyage, the settlement, defeat and triumph and reconciliation: all our ancestors are present in us. The archetypes are set, that make us human. But a new child for all that is a "*tabula rasa*"; first sounds and sights and comfortings and chidings are enormously important. He has brought the archetypes into time; he proceeds, with what time gives him, to make new unique patterns of them. It is all mime and play to begin with; but he must, whatever happens to him, force all the remaining flux of his life into those fixed patterns. In adolescence, maturity, age, the recurrent drama of "the free individual" and "the ancestral mask" may yield a great deal of suffering and joy, as well as half-remembered sweetnesses ("the children in the apple-tree"...). In this age of Prufrock and Bloom few lives rise to the grandeur of tragedy.

Perhaps if the little common siftings of dust that are our lives could be viewed with an all-compassionate eye, the proving of the grains might have more value than we expect.

But then, God is out of fashion these days, too. There is only the dust with brief breath in it.

Stromness in Orkney is a small seaport that first began to take shape in the late seventeenth century. About that time the trade of Europe was beginning to expand, with larger ships and richer markets; the American colonies were a whole new world for the merchants of the old world to exploit. For the ships of western Europe, often storm-battered between the North Sea and the half-charted Atlantic, the harbour of Stromness was a place of certain refuge and replenishment. Inns were built, country-folk came to the hamlet in the south-west with eggs and cheese and small pigs for sale. Fishermen signed on for the merchant ships and the whaling ships. A few astute lairds thought of laying their own keels, and trading richly into the Baltic. It was a bustling time in this part of Orkney. Parcels of land were bought along one side of the bay, and the owners crammed as many houses as they could on to their little enclosures, or 'quoys'. Half of Stromness stands out in the harbour; other foundations were dug out of the granite hill that shelters the town westwards. The whole complex was thrown together hurriedly, without plan or aesthetic consideration, yet the overall impression is of an inspired improvisation. (A pearl gets shaken now and then from an ordinary-looking oyster.)

Stromness has changed little from the eighteenth-century seaport. It is larger and quieter now. The single narrow surging twisting street is no longer thronged with men from the Davis Straits, and Dutch herring fishers. The old throbbing nerve of adventure and peril by sea is dead. There are no longer thirty-eight ale-houses up closes and down piers. The only busy time now is summer, when thousands of tourists take over the town. Yet the memory of that century of turbulence and prosperity is grained into the stones, and into the imagination of the townsfolk.

In this beautiful place I was born in 1921, in a corner house whose upstairs window looked out over the street and whose door opened on to a fisherman's pier. Twice a day the sea comes and goes about the steps and the slipway of Cloustons pier: a blue-and-gray brimming, an ebb that leaves desolations of heaped red seaweed.

My mother and father, sister and brothers, were presences that had been there always. Everything and everybody around me were at once ordinary and marvellous. I sat on the

11

doorstep among gulls and feet coming and going. Every day was an eternity. The sun shone. There were raindrops on the window-pane, and wind whined in the chimney. At night the paraffin lamp was lit on the table. My mother was always there, a kind environing presence. My father came and went, my brothers came and went more boisterously and unpredictably. There were fish and milk and bread on the table. Neighbours came with, to me, incomprehensible news, and were listened to by my mother with forbearance or wonderment; but to a young child it was only a strange music struck on the harp of the mouth. This is the first circle of a child's experience; everything is as it should be, all time is held in the cell of a single day.

The circle expands with walking and first words. My mother used to go shopping on a Saturday evening, with me at her coat-tails. The large bespectacled white-aproned grocer would bend down and say kind teasing words and put a sweetie in my red pout of a mouth. (I loved sweeties far more than the porridge and broth and mince-and-tatties I was forced to nibble at, with coaxings and gentle threatenings.) On the way home from the shops the windows along the street were all lighted. At the foot of the Church Road the Salvation Army stood in a ring – shining sonorous trumpet, merry melodion, tinkling tambourine, voices plaintive and sweet. We would linger there for a minute or two.

Perhaps we would meet my father on the street, a lantern pinned to his coat, a bunch of letters in his hand. He was a postman. I was given a ha'penny to spend myself: on sweeties, of course, in Janetta Sinclair's.

In the daytime my father sat on a wooden bench in the tailor shop, among bits of cloth, shears, iron 'geese', squares of chalk, lumps of resin, spools of dark thread. A needle shone between his fingers. Peter Esson and Willie Esson sat at other parts of the bench, cutting and stitching. My father was a

part-time tailor as well as a postman. They stopped their
adult talk when I came in from our house across the street;
their mouths were full then of words kind, teasing, half-
serious. The shop window was stuck with bills, announcing
cinema shows, church services, auction sales.

I liked Peter Esson's shop – a cloth-smelling cave.

Presently an old man would come in and sit on the bench
and tell a piece of street news: a fragment from some legend.

Word, language, story – the child breaks into another
marvellous circle of experience; though, to be sure, he takes it
all as his due.

My only sister was ten years older than me. She had the gift
of story-telling, and she could put the narrative across with
great emphasis and style. She seemed to practise her gift on
me alone; perhaps I was the only one who would listen. She
was at the age when love-stories appeal, and so I became an
enthralled witness to the emotional entanglements, generally
tragic, of young men and young women. Always the girls in
the end "died of a broken heart"; either because she was
deserted by her lover, or else, like Willie in Yarrow, he was
drowned coming to the love-tryst. I was very much impressed
by that image: the girl on the river-bank seeing her lover's cap
floating in the stream, and knowing then that she had lost him
forever ... Of course I had no conception of what this all-
important state of mind called 'love' was, but I accepted it as
an essential mysterious part of every story. The breaking of
the heart was a wistful beautiful satisfying way to die, I
supposed.

No doubt these early seeds of narrative and poetry lie
buried in a child's mind until, a quarter of a century or so
later, they began to stir and throb. (I think it was more a
rhythm and tone that were established – the characters and
actions in my sister's stories were quite unrelated to the life all
around us.) I could not imagine that the saddler in the shop
round the corner would ever be in a story – or the whispering
nodding women at the close-end – or the fisherman who sat on

13

his black-tarred box all day making and mending creels – or the canny apple-cheeked farmers who came in with their beasts to the mart on a Wednesday afternoon.

We were common dust. The story took place in a mysterious secure region that had its own timeless setting and laws.

And yet I, coming and going – and never venturing very far from my mother's door – was absorbing into my imagination the whole life of the little town: the man who swept the flagstones of the street; the one-eyed bell-ringer; the fishermen selling haddocks from a barrow; the milkmen with their horses and carts and huge metal churns; the magical lamplighter; the important men of the town, bailies and retired sea-captains and elders, who seemed so grave as they moved down the street in sombre suits; the Italian ice-cream man with chopped speech; the two fearful policemen pacing along side by side; the black-smudged coalman. Also the town in the twenties was full of zanies and eccentrics (the man who thought he was a ship, the washer-woman who danced and sang at certain places along the street) ... The important thing for me was that it was all play – people behaved that way because it had been set down for them, there was nothing else they could do. All were engaged in some strange game that would go on and on for ever with the same characters and the same setting. (I knew, theoretically, about birth and death – I would be shown new babies from time to time, with blind grimacing faces – three or four times a year my mother drew down the blind as the black horse-drawn funeral hearse went past with its coffin; but these also, the infant and the corpse, were a part of the endless round of make-believe.)

Solemnly, twice a year, the minister called, and drank tea in a grave unctuous calm ...

Once I was out in the street alone. A few drunk trawlermen from Aberdeen came lurching round a corner. I ran home in terror. (In those days Stromness had no pubs; the town had seen such wild splurges in the days of its prosperity that the women and "the kirk folk" had voted it dry the very year I was born.) I could not understand the speech and wild gestures of the strangers: they seemed to be frightening creatures who had no part in our story.

Another time I was sitting on the front doorstep when 'a travelling woman' arrived with her pack. She seemed so unutterably strange, in language and appearance, that I fainted clean away on the spot.

These experiences left marks on the mind. 'The drunk' and 'the tinker' move through nearly all my stories and plays and poems; symbolical figures who are both in and out of the story, for they (unlike the grocer, the minister, the policemen, the gossip, the fisherman) are not bound to one part forever but come and go at their own wild sweet will.

On the pier the fisherman sat, stringing his creels or coiling lines; or he pushed his silver-heaped barrow along the street among the mewling cats and wives, and stopped here and there to weigh haddocks on a little brass hand-scale, threepence per pound. I don't know when I began to think of him (there were several fishermen) as the essence of the town, the man bringing in the sea treasures, as the very first men on this shore had done. The fisherman became a symbol, but only much later. (Symbols are made when daily life is seen no longer as a mime, or a game, but as a perilous enduring between birth and death. Then the fisherman, as the original food-gatherer, the hunter in the sea, assumes an importance not usually accorded to him by men more safely circumstanced.)

Once every year, for a family outing, my father hired a car and we drove into the country. We visited two farms, one in Birsay where we had dinner, a large delicious pot of stewed cock chickens and mealy potatoes. Late in the afternoon we drove to another farm in Evie, where the table was spread with home-made jams, scones, cakes, butter, cheese. What impressed me in those farms, besides the gentle courtesy and kindness of the people themselves, was a sense of enormous stability. (Some of the Orkney farms have been worked by the same family for centuries.) To the child the farm-folk were also caught up in the inevitable story. But I had the obscure feeling that they played more ancient mysterious parts than the drapers, the sweetie-wives, and the magistrates of Stromness.

Fisherman and farmer are in a sense stark opposites. One is thirled to a perilous unpredictable element, which is sometimes generous and sometimes stingy (always menacing). The other is bound to the slow sure wheel of agriculture, which to be sure has its good and its bad years; but the steethe-stone is steadfast in the glebe. The Orkney crofters were poor in former generations; most of them had fishing yawls as well as plough-and-horse. Land and sea meshed in the one food-provider; a fish-oil lamp lit the table of bere-bannocks, cheese and ale.

Without that symbolical figure, the Orkney crofter with a boat, I think I could not have written a word of any significance.

The last grim circle before one grows up is 'school'. I never liked school from the first day. My mother used to tell me in later life how I came home after the first morning there, threw the little satchel in a corner, and said flatly, "That's that – I'm never going back there again! ..." (But even children of five have to obey the law – I was driven or cajoled schoolwards on subsequent mornings until it became a drab habit.)

The Scottish education system was a true child of the age that conceived it. Perhaps a form of idealism entered into it: educate *all* the children, and you will eliminate thereby much of the drabness, poverty, ignorance, crime that is such a stain on the industrial age. When a man can read and count and understand something of the large world around him, he is half-way free of his chains. Something like this, no doubt, was believed by some of the people who conceived the idea of universal education. Every child was to be given an opportunity to better himself. This Smilesian philosophy was implicitly believed in by almost everybody when I was a boy. We are here "to get on", to improve ourselves, to rise in the world. My father was a half-believer in this creed; often he would mention with admiration some poor boy from a croft who had done well in Edinburgh or further afield (like Dr John Gunn, who became a publisher and editor and author of many boys' books: my father either remembered or had been told about him going to school on bare feet, with a peat under his arm). There weren't many books in our house, but a few of them were of the improving kind – I remember the fictional biography of an American president called *From Log Cabin to White House* ... My father was an intelligent man who knew he was stuck forever to his post round and the tailor's bench; he hoped, maybe forlornly, that some of his children might, by means of education, rise a bit higher in the world, and be free of the money worries that perpetually harassed him. Yet he was a complex man; he hated any kind of upstart pretension. He would say often to us children, "Don't get above yourselves, whatever happens" ... He would quote Bunyan:

> He that is down need fear no fall,
> He that is low, no pride,
> He that is humble ever shall
> Have God to be his guide.

I am not sure about my father's early days before he got married. He sailed once to Labrador on a missionary ship. He had been to London and Glasgow, and he was appalled and fascinated for the rest of his life by the wretchedness of the slums there. (Poverty in Orkney, which everybody shared, was simple and noble in comparison.) These experiences, whatever they were, had moved him to a life-long compassion. The books he loved most of all were Jack London's novels – I think one of them, about the poor of London, was called *People of the Abyss*. Another of his favourite authors was an Irishman

17

who had settled in Glasgow, Patrick McGill, author of *The Rat-Pit* and *Children of the Dead End*. Another was *The Ragged Trousered Philanthropists*. He read these books over and over.

He was religious, in a kind of unquestioning way that brooked no argument. The Presbyterian establishment of our town did not appeal to him, though every Sunday regularly he herded the family gently to "the kirk". His great religious hero was William Booth, founder of the Salvation Army. He had heard Booth preaching in Glasgow, twice in one day, and it was an experience he never forgot. Booth's work among the poor of London was no doubt what principally impressed my father.

It must have seemed to him also that education would give some kind of dignity to the lives of all poor people, and bring in the end a measure of economic freedom; but beyond that modest right of every man, sat Dives among his goblets, gold, and honeyed bread; and that was abomination ... We must never, meantime, forget our simple origins ...

It was never openly said in class-room or assembly hall, that I remember; but still it was implicitly conveyed to us that a crofter or a fisherman was much lower in the scale of human worth than, for example, a shopkeeper or a man who wrote in ledgers in an office; and those humble food-gatherers were not to be compared in any way with lawyers, doctors, teachers, ministers, master mariners. (Beyond these, of course, in cities and places of importance, existed a vast hierarchy of wealth and privilege that the likes of us could wonder at, but never touch.)

It is easy to over-simplify. The country districts of Orkney have from the Norse beginnings nurtured people of high intelligence. Once the door was opened to them by the Education Act of 1872, there was an astonishing quickening. Round about the turn of the century Kirkwall Grammar School especially burgeoned with talent: Orkney seemed to breed professors who took their talents all over the Empire. Without that famous Act, would most of them have been

18

bound all their lives to croft and boat: mild eccentrics who speculated about stars, tides, the diverse atoms of peatbog and tilth and rock (there have always been a few like these, deprived of more advanced education)? It's impossible to say. Perhaps the intellectual curiosity of earlier Orkneymen took them to the Hudson's Bay and the colonies, while their more docile contemporaries stayed at home.

The best that we could hope for, from school, was to become at least literate tradesmen, shopkeepers who could balance figures in a ledger; something beyond mire and dung and seaslime. The clever ones, who won the class medal week after week, might go to Moray House in the end, or become a clerk in a lawyer's office.

To this end the huge gray unimaginative machine took us and tried to mould us. Instead of "magic casements opening on the foam", geography (for example) seemed to be all about the imports and exports of Brazil, Norway, etc. History was a catalogue of kings and battles (I must say how much I revelled in that). Maths was fractions, decimals, the endless litanies of the multiplication tables. For art, we spent gray hours drawing a jug with a duster draped about it. Music was ear-tests; occasionally, for refreshment, singing ("Sir Eglamore, that worthy knight" ... "See afar yon hill Ardmore".) Worst of all, for me, was the way the English language – which I instinctively loved, though I didn't know it at the time – was wrenched and tortured on the racks of 'analysis' and 'parsing'. There was even a period called 'drill', which seems, looking back, to have been the most vacuously conceived of all. There, in a hideous hall with a concrete floor, a young lady teacher took us through all kinds of artificial spasmodic exercises; as though children in our circumstances were not already perfectly fit and healthy with the wild sweet freedom that sea and hill gave us in our own free time.

For Religious Education our teacher would read to us stories out of the Old Testament – Joseph and his brothers, Noah's Ark, the wanderings of Abraham, Jacob and Esau and the inheritance. I listened to these, entranced; they still seem to me to be among the greatest stories of the world. (To me, a boy of eight or nine, they were simply stories; but I'm sure now that I was absorbing, all unconsciously, form and rhythm and texture.)

Another oasis in the school week for me was the period called 'composition'. The subjects we were given to write about were often ridiculous – "A Day in the Life of a Gamekeeper" or "The Autobiography of a Tree". Why was it, when all around me my fellow-pupils were sweating and groaning to get a few more words out, the sentences and paragraphs flowed eagerly from my pen? Nearly always, every week, I had written the best essay. I couldn't understand it then; the work seemed sweet and effortless as a flower opening. (I realize now, with gratitude, that it was the one talent I had been given. I have tried, as best I can, to develop it; if I didn't have it to work on, I would be a life-long lingerer at the pier-head; for, except being perhaps a clerk in an office, there was nothing else I could do.) I had not the courage or sea-wit to be a fisherman.

Experience of that futile five-days-a-week round has bred a new race of more enlightened educationalists; children nowadays actually look forward to their classes, for some of them the summer holiday is too long. School is no longer "the shades of the prison house" that my generation knew.

Many of our teachers were kind and good people; they were as much victims of the system as we were.

It is a pity that universal education was rooted in the Victorian age, with all its notions of stern duty, self-help, and the sacredness of possessions. I think, perhaps romantically, that childhood should be an extended play-time (with allowances made for the private life to which every child is entitled). After the necessary discipline of the alphabet and numbers, it should be all stories, plays, music, the making of patterns. It is only through these gateways of delight that knowledge of the world ought to come, and experience take

20

over at last from innocence.

For me, at any rate, that kind of education would have been the best.

Meantime, the elements of my first childhood, that had seemed so ordinary, gradually over many years became a setting for the ancient rituals to be enacted once again: it was under these ordinary skies that the hunt, the battle, the voyage, the settlement, the triumph and defeat and reconciliation, take place; and the men and women and children of the islands (and everywhere) are the eternal actors. It is the writer's task to relate the legend (what Edwin Muir called "the fable") to this age of television, uranium, and planet-flight.

SELECTED BIBLIOGRAPHY

A Time to Keep (1969); *Greenvoe* (1972); *Magnus* (1973); *A Spell for Green Corn* (1970); *An Orkney Tapestry* (1969); *Selected Poems* (1977).

2. The Boy on the Roof

by George Bruce

George Bruce was born in 1909 in Fraserburgh, Aberdeenshire. His first collection of poetry was Sea Talk, *published in 1944. This book was followed by* Scottish Sculpture Today *(1946) in which he collaborated with the sculptor, T.S. Halliday. After some years as a teacher of English he was, from 1946 to 1970, a BBC producer in Aberdeen and Edinburgh. In 1971 he became the first Fellow in Creative Writing at Glasgow University, and on demitting this post in 1973 he held various short-term appointments at American colleges and universities which took him from Virginia to Arizona. His most recent appointment was Visiting Professor of English at the College of Wooster, Ohio, from 1976–1977.*

I must have been four or five years old when an episode occurred, which, against what I regarded as my better judgement, projected itself into a poem just over a quarter of a century later.

Our house, 2 Victoria Street, Fraserburgh – the house where I was born – was granite, white granite, as I recollect. It sparkled in the sun. The big front door was oak. We faced north. To the north the town was bounded by the Moray Firth, and between us and it was the major part of the town of ten thousand inhabitants. To the east, little more than quarter of a mile away was the North Sea or German Ocean. Unless you climbed on the roof (which I did, to the inexplicable

23

distress of Mrs Benzie, an important, polite lady who happened to be passing) you could not see the sea, but on that promontory of the land of Buchan, the north-east corner of Aberdeenshire, it made its presence felt all the time. The sun rose over the sea and it set over it. You could smell it, and you could taste its salt on your lips. Its sound was so customarily in your ears that you never heard it, but became the more aware of it when unusually it fell silent. The occasion to which I have referred related to this condition.

Half-way up the stairs of the house is a landing. It is lit by a window of frosted glass, of Gothic style so large that it reaches from the landing to the ceiling of the second floor. It was possible to stand on the low, deep window-sill, behind a dark curtain which was draped almost from the ceiling to the floor, and then jump out on an unsuspecting child. This fun backfired on me, because after dark I became fearful of going upstairs. My fear was greatly intensified after I was told part of a story by an old woman who was 'baby-sitting' for our parents on a stormy night. She had reached the climax of the tale, when the return of our parents – there were two of us, my brother and I – caused her to break off. By the following night the winds had ceased, and a thick mist had settled on the town, though the waters continued to roar. Little wonder that when years later I read the lines in *Thomas the Rhymer*:

> And they saw neither sun nor moon,
> But they heard the roaring of the sea.

I recognised that Thomas was at the place where awe and fear meet, for I had been there, was there without stirring a foot outside our strong house. I was convinced, on that evening, that the solution to the unfinished tale lay behind the curtain waiting for my approach, and that I would never reach my bedroom on the north-east corner of the house. I put up all sorts of excuses to my mother for not going upstairs. Then just when I was on the point of being compelled to face death, there was a peremptory ringing and noise at the front door, to which we both went, and there stood my father. He said: "A boat has gone." I should say rather that I presume he said the conventional phrase, for my only recollection is of the immediate disappearance of my misery and its replacement by a wave of happiness; all my imaginary fears vanished while he told of the realities of some who survived and of some who were drowned as a result of the skipper of a boat mistaking the bay in the fog for the entrance to the harbour. The beach slopes gently in the bay. Before the breeches buoy could be set up my father and other men had formed a life-chain and had rescued some of the crew. This is the poem which came out of the episode, which I wrote, I think early in 1940. "The Curtain".

Half way up the stairs
Is the tall curtain.
We noticed it there
After the unfinished tale.

My father came home,
His clothes sea-wet,
His breath cold.
He said a boat had gone.

He held a lantern.
The mist moved in,
Rested on the stone step
And hung above the floor.

I remembered
The blue glint
Of the herring scales
Fixed in the mat,

And also a foolish crab
That held his own pincers fast.
We called him
Old Iron-clad.

I smelt again
The kippers cooked in oak ash.
That helped me to forget
The tall curtain.

When I wrote that poem I was as far from seeking a mystery as was the child whom I must have been. He sought for objects which defined themselves, which had their own independent existence, which could be seen and touched, as could the herring scales, which became fixed in the mat after my father had come from the yard, where the herring were cured, with the scales on the soles of his boots. Held to the light, little blue lights danced through their transparencies. They were like sequins, though I would not have known what these were at the time. All these things gave their pleasure, I believe, because they existed for the child within the security of the love our parents had for each other, from which grew affection and understanding for their children.

One may wonder with hindsight why the use of such an inheritance for poetry should be in doubt, but if the direction of urban society and the direction of the new literature of the twenties and thirties be considered, then to allow the imagination to dwell on locations and events of very marginal consequence to that society appeared to me as tantamount to intellectual dishonesty. The deleterious consequences to poetry due to the week-end country visitations of the Georgian Poets of the 'Why do you walk through the fields in gloves?' school, was very evident by the early thirties when the sense of a fragmenting and decaying society had been conveyed in an appropriate style in Eliot's *The Waste Land*, and when the most trustworthy assurances for me were in the subjective universes of Joyce and Virginia Woolf. With many others I saw the approaching cataclysm of war as the nadir preordained by the disappearance of a personal society before the rapid advance of a mechanistic society which equated progress with financial profit. I recollect identifying myself with the fragile, intense, glowing world of Virginia Woolf's *To the Lighthouse*, and going from there to Pound's *Hugh Selwyn Mauberley*, to listen over and over to such lines as:

> The 'age demanded' chiefly a mould in plaster,
> Made with no loss of time,
> A prose kinema, not, not assuredly, alabaster
> Or the 'sculpture' of rhyme.

To apply one's ear to the sensitive formal verse of Pound especially as it was applied to the gross banalities of our day seemed to me the necessary thing to do: and when the images from the dark and dingy streets of Dundee, where I was a teacher in 1939, particularly on a night in December were a drunk falling out of a shop door-way and a woman offering herself, the necessary material seemed to be arranging itself for a statement in verse. And this I attempted to set down on the short train journey over the Tay Bridge to my home in Wormit in Fife. Yet by the time I was at the other side of the river I was writing on a different subject matter, one which insisted that in Scotland, at least, objects and persons still by merely existing gave cause for praise. One could not praise in terms of the exploited and commercialised language of the 'heart', nor could I come to terms with the introverted interests of the Aberdeenshire dialect, which had become a vehicle for the cosy nostalgia of Charles Murray. I began with the laconic statement of "My House".

> My house
> Is granite
> It fronts
> North,

> Where the Firth flows,
> East the sea.
> My room
> holds the first

Blow from the North,
The first from the East,
Salt upon
The pane.

The wind that blew through the verses in Scots or English in Aberdeenshire had no salt in it, for all those in Aberdeenshire who had written before me in Scots or English were landward writers. The home of the great majority was "yon broad Buchan land", as John C. Milne, the most exact observer of all the Aberdeenshire dialect writers, described the wide terrain, which spreads northwards from Aberdeen with only slight undulations till eight miles from Fraserburgh it rises to our only landmark, Mormond Hill, seven hundred and sixty nine feet above sea-level, or their eyes were on the more distinguished feature to the west of the shire, "the tap o' Bennachie", which rises to just under 1700 feet. Nothing suited their purpose better to describe that locality than "the bonnie dialect" (to quote John C. Milne again) which the farming folk used and which the poets used with feeling. It was a tongue which acknowledged the pull and suck of the earth in the tempo of its rhythms. The feet of the ploughman must plod, but there is no plodding in the nimble feet of the fisherman. Necessity demanded agility and balance. Yet such is the unconscious pressure of custom that the idea which presented itself to me about the people of Aberdeenshire was of a 'kindly folk' who sang their local songs (sangies) as they went about their domestic business. Such a view was marginal to my childhood. The distinguishing feature of an upbringing in the town where the sea thundered its blessings and curses was the presence of an absolute. Whereas each piece of landscape draws attention by its difference from any other to locality, the sea proclaims its universality. So a dialect, with its local references, might well be appropriate in its suggestion of difference, but I required for my purposes a different instrument.

I think I was fortunate in not discovering my 'objective co-relative' until I had been subjected to that 'purifying of the language of the tribe' to adapt Pound's phrase, which that master considered to be one of the functions of poetry. Perhaps that world of stone, air, light, and dark could only have become known and its experiences available at the point I heard the special merit in the phrase: "A boat has gone." That phrase had already been purified, not by the poet, but by a community which required a spare, athletic language for survival's sake, and in this case words which would convey terrible news quickly and with a minimum of emotion. Such a phrase puts the writer in the right place, that is to say out of the way so that the light can shine through the words, so that the thing itself speaks. Just how right these words were I discovered in 1974, when a student at Prescott College, Arizona after hearing me read "The Curtain" presented my wife with a poem he had written entitled "A Boat done Gone". Gary Moodie's grandfather had been a bay fisherman in the Gulf of Mexico, and in the village in Texas, where he lived this was the common phrase to express that loss. My meeting with Gary Moodie was an odd chance which no longer looks like chance for it linked with a habit of seeing and moving that developed inevitably in my childhood.

Day in, day out for some two to three weeks I watched, in the brilliant February Arizona morning, from a window which looked across desert country far wider than Buchan, a figure on horseback appear from behind a massif, black against the sun, and then make its way to Prescott College Campus. I noticed the pliant movement of the body as it responded to the rhythm of the horse. I could not help but compare the secure, yet fluent poise to that of the fisherman, whom I would watch when a boy, as sometimes with hands in pockets he stood at ease balancing against the rise and fall of the swell on the shifting deck as if boat and man and sea were all part of a single rhythm of nature. In a lecture I made this comparison, remarking that the rider appeared to be riding bare-back, but he was too far off to say for certain. That night the rider Gary Moodie, who had unknown to me attended the lecture, appeared at the door. He said: "I thought you'd like to meet my red mustang." The horse was not broken in. They had made their way together through New Mexico and so to Arizona. Many years ago I believed that such intimate relationships, man and boat, man and horse, all those out of which personal societies grew, like that in which Robert Burns lived, must become things of the past, and that we had to learn to live in a more highly organised, though less integrated society. Now there is evidence of revolt against the conditions where no integrating rhythm of life may be felt, where the individual feels there is no connection between his thoughts and wishes and what he finds himself compelled to do by social conditions. A true poem in so far as it is one thing is a paradigm of the relation which man desires to have with his society, for it is complete in itself and yet includes events from the incompleteness of life. Rilke's poem, "The Spanish Trilogy", begins with a supplication that out of disparate phenomena – the cloud, hill, night wind, river, "and out of me", one thing be made. The poem reaches a climax in a tribute to a shepherd, because despite his having "world in every upward glance, in every bending" his identity was not threatened. The threat to identity could, of course, only be felt by the isolated poet. How much more strongly, it seems to me, the integrity of the fisherman is threatened, in his daily confrontation with the element which is his preserver and destroyer, than that of the shepherd.

When I write 'the fisherman' I have a particular man in mind. When I was a child I was taken to many fishermen's houses in the villages of Broadsea, which became part of Fraserburgh, and of Cairnbulg, which lay across the three miles stretch of sand on a bow bend. Their houses were dark inside. The windows were kept tight shut. My father, as effective head of the herring-curing firm of A. Bruce and Company, the oldest firm in the North-East of Scotland, visited the cottages to ask the wives or daughters of the fishermen to gut the herring during the summer fishing season in Fraserburgh or to engage them to travel south to Great Yarmouth for the autumn fishing. Wherever we went there was always a feeling of welcome, even as there was when I went aboard the drifters in the harbour, where again I felt the dark come upon me as we went below decks. One other image comes to mind in this context. For no known reason I had gone to the beach and was looking across the bow bend on a fine Sunday morning, when at the far end of the arc I noticed a grouping of black dots which became people, who were walking on the sands towards the town. As they came nearer – there must have been well over a hundred – I became aware of an odd effect. Their dark blue trouser clad legs seemed to stop short of the sand, so that they did not appear to be walking at all, but simply moving above ground level and level with a quiet sea. When they reached the edge of the sands, before crossing the green links which run from the sands to the town, I saw their bare feet on to which they were putting their socks and their boots, which they had carried over their shoulders. When I got home I began to doubt what I had seen though the reason for their journey was common enough. They were going to the Baptist or Congregational Church in Fraserburgh. The doubt arose because I heard no sound from the fishermen. Was it that the sound of the sea (which, as I mentioned, we did not hear because it was our silence) covered their conversation, or was it that their lives being responsive to each necessity as it arose, there was no occasion for speech.

Suddenly I found my business as writer in the nineteen-forties was to set down such facts, and the sense of the facts but this could only be presented in rhythms which were controlled and free. When I wrote "The Fishermen" I did not have in mind his symbolic implications. He was a man leaving his home for his boat. This is the poem:

As he comes from one of those small houses
Set within the curve of the low cliff
For a moment he pauses
Foot on step at the low lintel
Before fronting wind and sun.
He carries out from within something of the dark
Concealed by heavy curtain,
Or held within the ship under hatches.

Yet with what assurance
The compact body moves,
Head pressed to wind,
His being at an angle.
As to anticipate the lurch of earth.

Who is he to contain night
And still walk stubborn
Holding the ground with light feet
And with a careless gait?
Perhaps a cataract of light floods
Perhaps the apostolic flame.
Whatever it may be
The road takes him from us.
Now the pier is his, now the tide.

Once the poem was on the page I saw the attraction of the
fisherman was in his being 'one thing' in the face of light and
dark, wind and water, that he contains night, even though the
light for him is momentary. On the north-east promontory
where there was room for the wind to howl and the eye was
bounded by the horizon line of the sea, everything stated itself
for what it was with complete clarity. The fisherman achieved
his perfect balance, 'his being at an angle' leaning into the
wind. It was a marvellous place for a boy. The elements
demanded expertise and energy. We had both.

The energy was in the ground and in the air. We merely
shared it. In "The Startled Hare" I wrote:

Hare leaps with eye of fear.
Sparse grass, sanded and salt, prompts.
And air – what daylight here!
Through limb and limb cavorts.

I started up that hare. I was running over the springy turf –
a mile of sheep pasture – the last lap of the walk which my
father had taken me to the Loch of Strathbeg, six miles to the
south of Fraserburgh, about which I wrote a poem. It begins:

Space! – here runs astringent air
Across the loch fixed
In three miles of flat,
The habitat of thistle and hare.

In the North-East the loch had to be fixed, held down, or it
would have been blown away. The last line of the poem is
"Tree torn from soil". Long before I wrote that kind of poem,
its date is 1940 or '41, certain words began to linger in my ear.
One was 'habitat': it bangs around. Your ear can't get out of
it. The sound sends you back to the beginning when you get to
the end of the word, a right kind of word for the place of my
birth. The town itself was absorbed, I felt, into the elements of
light and air and water. I wrote of it:

Between the flat land of the plain
And the brief rock – the town.
This morning the eye receives
(As if space had not intervened,
As if white light of extraordinary transparency
Had conveyed it silently and with smooth vigour)
The granite edge, edifice of stone –
The new tenement takes the sun.

The shop fronts stare,
The church spire signals heaven,
The blue tarred streets divide and open sea-ward,
The air leaps like an animal.

33

Did once the sea engulf all here and then
At second thought withdraw to leave
A sea-washed town?

The incorporation of the elements into the composition of the town is not just due to the fluidity of memory and imagination. The intensity of the light in the North-East has been verified by light meter readings of photographers. The impact of the wind needs no verification. When I read Wordsworth's line in *The Prelude*, "When we had given our bodies to the wind", I knew he was talking about the experts all boys are, given the right conditions, such as those we had.

We gave our bodies not only to the wind but to the sea. At any moment when you were with other boys on the beach somebody would say: "Let's go for a dook," and our clothes would drop from us and we were in stark naked. The great thing was to time your entry under water exactly as the wave was breaking, and still more expertly assess the strength of the undertow so that you knew how much breath was required when you allowed yourself to be pulled under. As for the goings on in the harbour, the dodging of the spray as it swept over the high breakwater which sheltered the main basins was fun, though with some danger in it, for often as not these great brilliant fans were preludes to the immediate arrival of lumps of water, which would have swept us into the harbour, but more interesting was crossing the partially built basin on planks and logs with vertical supports to bring them to the level of the stone piers. There were gaps between the planks, and they narrowed to barely more than a foot's breadth. My father caught me at this and he took me round the several piers saying: "You can fall in there," till he came to one where he said severely: "But not here." At that point the water was shallow. Had I slipped I would have cut my head on the rocks beneath the water. The ravings of the wind and the roaring of waters were ours. No game of football was ever called off because of weather. I remember when one of our backs in a

Fraserburgh Academy team playing (I think) Buckie
Academy lashed the ball only to see it blown back over his
head and swerve past our goal-keeper. Of course we went to
school, but what went on there was kept in its place, by the
more significant education of our bodies and minds that went
on, unknown to us, outside.

That is too unqualified as statement. We learned reading
and writing and arithmetic and history and geography at the
Central Public School, the name of which was carved in large
capitals on the granite building. Another credit to that school
was the healthy disrespect for authority which we learned,
thanks to Colonel Reid's disciplinary methods. He, the
headmaster, saw to it that we kept in line previous to our
entering the building by lashing at our legs with a leather
thong. So he confirmed the community of boyhood. We knew
that balancing our bodies in the wind, running barefoot
rhythmically and freely on the shore was what mattered. In
school we did 'drill' in the playground – "Quick march!
Heads up, chests out. One, two, one two." It may have had
something to do with the army. It had nothing to do with life.
But that other rhythm was another matter. I wrote:

We were the shabby boys that edged the beach
Till night and watched the sea-light fail,
The sand blow draughty through our legs
And coil in puffs and leap and fall,
We blowing on our blue hands
And stamping on the shore.

Whereas the rigidities of school disciplines could be isolated
from living, into the mere business of running and jumping
and even fighting slipped apprehensions unsought and
unacknowledged. Saturday night was the great night for boys,
especially in summer when the stalls, shouds (swings),
roundabouts, chair-o-planes and booths were set up on the
northern edge of the links which bordered the town. The
boxing booth was a great attraction when Deef Burke was

there taking on all comers. My poem, "A Boy's Saturday Night", ends:

Here Rob Burke was at work
Taking all comers
Till dark.
He put the finger of his glove

To his flat nose, snorted,
And then spat.
Short work was made of
Our Tom Scott.

We saw even the dust rise.
Outside the land was black.
"That's queer," I said,
"Sea's lit – like a lamp".

I had gone to watch a bloody battle, if need be by scrambling on my belly under the tent canvas, but the environment in which the battles were enacted did not allow the focus of the boy's mind to be limited by his purposes. Suddenly, for dark had fallen, he discovered he was part of a strange, new world; a mysterious unknown was included in his vision. It was art and part of both the intense drama – the figure of the father at the door was edged in mist – and of mundane activities.

The way of life of the Bruces simply by virtue of the role they played in the community was incorporative, but the individuality of members of the family, took their physical and mental interests beyond what might have been expected. Even so no one should remember that Fraserburgh once had a university. Built in 1595 it lasted no longer than the tenure of its first Principal who was thrown into jail under the orders of James VI and I, for disputing the King's ecclesiastical authority. The act of the Principal was characteristic of the Fraserburgh tradition of putting to the test of good sense whatever authority ordained. If there was no sense in the law then one should get round it, but first the matter must be debated. I think I inherited a tradition of belief in the importance of service to the community and also of belief in the individual's right to go his own way provided this did not disrupt the community. I am not sure how far this applies to my great-grandfather's management of his cooperage, which he worked from Cairnbulg towards the end of the eighteenth century, a subsidiary aspect of which, tradition has it, was the supplying of barrels for smuggled hollands gin, stored conveniently under the minister's stair. His house, which I would have passed on the way to the Loch of Strathbeg, was pointed out to me by a fisherman as "the big house over there" (it was inland from the village), "and ye'll know the house next to it was the Greig's". He went on to say that the Greigs changed their name to Grieg when they emigrated to Norway – that is Grieg the composer's ancestors.

Today everyone gets classified. We are business men, or professional people, or 'working class' or whatever. In Fraserburgh we got on with a kind of living which absorbed a wide range of experience which we didn't bother to classify. Now looking back one sees there were traditions of interests in music, in poetry – my grandmother used to arrange for Mr Browning's new poetry to be sent immediately from London so that it could be read and discussed at her informal gatherings. As for art – there was hardly a room in our house which was not hung with water colours of faint unstormy seas, many by my mother, some by my father's elder brother, Charles, who used to go out on sketching expeditions with a man called George Reid, who turned out to be President of the Royal Scottish Academy. It was characteristic of the Bruce spread of interests that the bed he occupied in the house of my grandfather, George Bruce, where he was put up, was occupied on the following night by General Booth of the Salvation Army. George Bruce began to preach around the country when he was seventy-five. By the time he was ninety, my father told me, he was nearing his best. His mind had

37

broadened, so that he recognised Catholics were Christians. None of this impinged directly on me.

An image swims out of my early childhood. A long procession of horses and carts are on their way to the country. Men, the employees of A. Bruce and Co., and women and children are on forms strapped to the floats. Everyone is dressed up for the occasion of the Bruces' Strawberry Drive, to be held at Cortes Loch, a sheltered wooded place, five miles from the town. Long tables, covered in white linen, are set out in the open. There seems to be hundreds of plates of strawberries, great jugs of cream and vast bowls of sugar. Everything is shining for it is a beautiful summer day. In business terms the picnic makes no sense. The Drive is being held during the height of the fishing season. "Just like the Bruces!"

"Fa echts ee?" (who owns you?) said a fisherman to me. I was down the harbour at the barking slip watching him at his nets. I told him that Harry Bruce was my father. He commented, "Ye were born wi a silver speen in yer mou". This extraordinary piece of information so engaged my attention that I paid no heed to the genealogy of the family which the fisherman was giving, until my ear caught another remark. "Wild girls," he said. He was referring to my girl cousins, who were all much older than me. This was no news – their exploits of leaping from boat to boat, diving off piers (Nesta had swum across Fraserburgh Bay), of riding in the street a penny-farthing bicycle, were known to me. But the remark linked with a rumour. They had been seen running around "in their bloomers!" There was a good reason for the disrobing, which I discovered when exploring a building in the curing-yard. There I found the Bruces' home-made gymnasium with a horse and mats, rings and ropes and other gymnastic appurtenances. This was where my father learned his gymnastic skills, which I observed as he swung on the rings of Pindar-Ord's Circus on the links one morning before a performance. His conscious interests in balance and control

38

had begun as a child in Germany. He was sent there at the age of ten to learn German – my grandfather had acquired friends in the Hamburg area through business – and he came back a skilled skater. So deeply did my grandfather feel for his German friends that he never got over the shock of the outbreak of war and, (according to my father) died as a result of it three months short of his hundredth birthday.

No doubt to start off with one objective and to acquire others in different fields is common enough, but in our case the related objectives through speculation or even need tended to intermingle, or in my case become the principal objective for a time, as when I, having applied for the post of Assistant Master in the English Department at the High School of Dundee, found myself within three days of my application being received, teaching physical education there, and therefore demonstrating balance and rhythmical control. I did not see the art of balance as separate from the art of reading poetry or listening to music. To be totally absorbed into, say a Beethoven sonata, is to become part of the expression of a being greater than one-self, and in this the effect is physical as well as aesthetic. Unfortunately usually one must dress up, affect certain dispositions, and travel to another place to achieve the experience and in so doing isolate it from one's usual living, but this was not the case for me in Fraserburgh.

Outside the gymnasium in the curing-yard the girls at the gutting would be singings songs in Gaelic, for many of them had come from the Hebrides, while at home a more powerful spell was exerted by my Auntie Vi as she played Beethoven on our Winkelmann. She preferred it to her own piano for its tones were more sonorous. By the age of eleven I had heard, I think, all the sonatas, listened to them on Saturday mornings and sometimes in the afternoon, though then I was on the horns of a dilemma for the drama of the Appasionata might be being enacted at the same time as Fraserburgh would be in contest with its great rival Peterhead. Our rotund mongrel, Spicey, a cross between a Skye terrier and something else had no problems. He attended the football matches. He had the catholicity of interests of the family. He went to the cinema every Friday evening. If no member of the family was present, an attendant put down a seat for him. He also never missed the chance of latching himself on to any funeral procession which was making its way to Kirkton Cemetery a mile or so from our house.

Kirkton Cemetery, where are buried my forefathers – some 130 years of them – lies in the lea of the bents, sandhills planted with marram grass to hold the sand in place, and a bulwark against the sea. But the sand spilled over the wall and spread itself on the flat tomb-stones, on one of which Brandy, a native whose name tells of his predilection, was awakened one morning by the grave-digger with the words, "Ye maun be gey cauld in that place, Brandy". To which Brandy responded, "Nae as cauld as the man aneath".

All these matters, the absurd and the profound, the accidental deaths at sea, the unexpected imaginative experiences in music and literature, such as my discovery of Byron's *Don Juan*, when I was eleven or twelve, were acceptable. (My hand reached out from my bed and found it in the bookshelves by my bed. So my introduction to sex had a comic bias, though later my father restored the balance by reading passages of D.H. Lawrence to us at the dinner-table.) One death, as a child, I could not accept.

One stormy November day my brother and I had gone to watch the spectacle of waves breaking over rocks, when I noticed a white body being swept into an inlet by a wave towards a rock and then being withdrawn at speed. Without far stronger help than either of us could give, I being about ten years old and my brother eight, he had no hope of survival. My brother said, "You wait: I'll go for the coastguards." I was shocked not simply by the boy's predicament, but by his being a local boy. To go bathing at any time of the year was natural, but a native who stripped and bathed in these conditions must have been out of his mind. He was betraying our intimate traditional knowledges. I stood and watched him till he drowned. Despite the recurrence of this image in my mind more than forty years were to pass before I could write it down, and then only after another death had strangely released it from censorship.

On a November or December evening in 1960 or '61 I entered a room in my home in Edinburgh in time to see on television a man running easily and loosely, yet quickly, turn and then drop in a heap. I wrote this immediately:

> He ran in the living air
> Exultation in his heels
> Earth thrust him upwards,
> Weightless – at that moment
> With large hands dangling loose
>
> A gust of wind will erect
> A twisting tower of dried leaves,
> That will collapse when
> The breath is withdrawn.
>
> He turned momentarily,
> His eyes looking into his fear,
> Seeking himself.
>
> When he fell the dust
> Rose in the air
> Like an empty container
> Of him.

The man was a peasant from Laos. The programme was a television war report. In the moment of his death in the manner of his running he showed he was of human kind. He was the fisherman in his momentary poised completeness, and he was myself. I seem unable to escape from making this kind of statement in rhythm about the short, exquisite and complete thing that life may become when you have learned to respond to it with your being. Then that being is enriched. In a moment I am the boy that I was and the man that I am now.

The boy who drowned in the storm drowned himself, depriving himself of the rich experience which life offered in Fraserburgh. I also witnessed in Fraserburgh a prodigal waste of the staff of life, a wanton destruction of herring, or so it seemed to me, and at a time when there were really poor people in Scotland. Our school holidays began at the end of June. The height of the summer fishing season was reached in the North-East in July. On one day in that month there had been heavy catches. The boats came in laden to the gunnels, only to find the market glutted; the prices offered by the herring curers were not enough to pay for the coal burned by the drifters to take them to the fishing grounds and back. When I arrived at the harbour, some boats had already put to sea, others were preparing to leave the port, all still laden with herring, which were to be dumped back in the sea. There was at least one heap of herring on the ground of a pier, a sight I had not seen before. A fisherwoman was making to pick up some of the herring when a skipper forbade her. Usually she would have paid a small price for herring which she would have put in her creel with other fish, and then gone to the country to sell the fish to farming people. I must have been about fifteen, the year 1924 or '25. I knew that children in Glasgow suffered from rickets owing to malnutrition. Why could not the herring be hurried in lorries there?

What I have described suddenly came back to me on account of a chance conjunction of two items which appeared in *The Scotsman* early in 1975. From looking on a photograph of two starving, refugee children on a road in South-East Asia, my eye went to a paragraph on the same page. It stated that owing to the serious depletion of herring stocks in the North Sea, all fishing for herring must cease from a given date. I wrote a poem, "On the Roads", which began in English:

Little children
walk
in their bones
on the roads.

The poem continues in Scots, as it refers to the episode in
the 1920s, since the skipper is presumed to be speaking to the
fisherwoman:

> There's nae eneuch bellies
> in the warld to feed.

And so on to the reverse picture of today:

> Says the man that kens:
> "Stop huntin thae herrin,

> There's nae eneuch herrin
> in a' the seas
> tae feed thae folk
> on the roads."

If my home-town were to provide images which were simply
a means of escape from the present, I would stop writing
about it, but the failure to share the available food, points to
an acute problem in this country today, the failure to share the
available work. It is self-evident that there should be no over-
time till all are at work, but this is to write with the assurance
of youth, an assurance which developed along with the
enjoyment of a physical control of the body, and which might
be associated with a taste for heights.

You may recollect that I began this essay as if I was on the
roof of 2 Victoria Street, and that I had failed to come down
despite Mrs Benzie. There was a marvellous view from beside
the chimney-pots. A vast expanse of sea, interrupted only by
the spire of the South Church pointing into a stationary blue
heaven, glittered to the north, the east and so south, and then
south-south west beyond a pattern of fields was the dark
brown of Mormond Hill.

> It's Mormond Braes where heather grows,
> Where oft-times I've been cheery,

goes the old song to a delightful lilt. At any moment, I felt, I might take wing. I looked down. Not only was Mrs Benzie looking up from the street, but there was also Mrs Thorburn and Mrs Watt and others, and as I looked my assurance ran out at the toes of my boots. Petrified I clung to the chimney-stack. The drama of my life had taken a wrong turning. "Don't move!" shouted my mother's head from a bedroom window. "They're coming with a ladder." The indignity of it – my father coming with a ladder. Indignation struggled with cowardice. I slipped down the far side and in through another bedroom window. A man came with a ladder, not my father. No doubt he was in his office, amused, probably thinking, "At least he got as far as the roof".

In *Scottish Poetry, Nine*, the last anthology of the series, the experience found its way into print. My poem, *Angels' Wings or Whatever* opens with:

When I was very young, a sprightly angular boy,
they were everywhere, but especially under my feet,
lifting me up – I went loping through the air,
(as all the Stars, football and female do now)
in slow motion – so I was captain of the football team.
They called me to the roof-tops and I climbed
in the dizzy air. It whisked about my big ears,
my nostrils gathered the sea-smell from far-away waters;
my eyes collected the bright beach and the rocking boats
in the little harbour at one go. I sat on the golden roof top.

SELECTED BIBLIOGRAPHY

Sea Talk (1944); *Collected Poems* (1970); *Anne Redpath* – a monograph of the Scottish painter (1974); *Festival in the North* – the story of the Edinburgh Festival (1975); *Some Practical Good* – the Cockburn Association, 100 years participation in the planning (1975).

3. Early Days in Edinburgh

by Robert Garioch

Robert Garioch was born at Edinburgh in 1909, to Scots-speaking parents, and graduated in English at the University of Edinburgh. The earliest contemporary influence was Poems in Two Tongues *by A.D. Mackie, and the first piece of literary good fortune was publication in the* Scots Observer *(in about 1933) of most of the poems in Scots as they were written, and of a weekly column about life in Edinburgh. In the past ten years or so as a retired teacher he has transcribed tape-recordings in the School of Scottish Studies and worked on the staff of the* Dictionary of the Older Scottish Tongue *as a lexicographer's orraman.*

I am proud of my parentage, but know little of my ancestors. Not being landed they would not vex themselves about family trees. My father was a painter, like his father before him. My mother was a music teacher, before she was married. Her father was a company porter in Leith Docks, discharging bulk cargoes of grain. The metters and weighers tipped it into a sack which was placed on the back of the porter, who carried it from the ship across a plank to the shed. My mother used to tell me the full sack weighed 2½cwt. My father's people had 'always' belonged to Edinburgh; my mother's were Mathewsons, hinds and grieves who circulated from one farm to another, never far from Kelso. My father was a violinist also, a fiddler, to use his own word, a semi-professional of the theatres and picture-houses; he would often come home from work to find himself required as a deputy, then he would clean himself and set off at a trot with his fiddle-case under his oxter, very pleased. My mother had taught the piano, also the mandoline and similar instruments. Miss Kate Mathewson's Mandoline Band was very popular. I have a programme of a concert in the Free Gardeners' Institute in Picardy Place, dated 1899, admission one shilling. Songs were to include "Daddy" and "The Storm Fiend"; mandoline solos would be "Alice, Where Art Thou?" played by Miss Bella Calder, and a Selection from "The Geisha" by Miss Mathewson. There were only two Scotch items on that programme, but that was unusual. This was the kind of music to which my infant ears were tuned.

My mother taught me the beginnings of piano-playing; later I had lessons from someone I regarded as a 'proper teacher', because he charged fees and I had to go to his house. These two teachers did me good service till I reached Form V at school and had to swot all the time, for fear of making a dog's breakfast of what we called the 'Leavings'. In the early thirties I was one of the last picture-house pianists, in the Lyric in Nicolson Square, the 'relief pianist' for twenty minutes each evening while the trio had their break, with Saturday matinées from two till six. I was paid fifteen shillings, which made me a rather well-off student, and I spent £8 on a second-hand motorbike from Guthrie in Hawick; for the *cognoscenti* I may add that it was a 1924 Douglas, 350 c.c., two gears, belt-drive, acetylene lights, no clutch, no kick-start. It carried me there and back to places all over Scotland many times, and to London one and a half times. Piano-playing became an obsession. I had two further periods of lessons, much later on, from very good teachers. I tried very hard, and spent much time that might have been used in reading and writing, till I reached the stage where many fail, foundering in the final coda of the Waldstein Sonata. To me, music and poetry are each of a somewhat similar nature. I do not like to hear metrical poetry read with more attention to full-stops than to line-endings, and hate to hear rhymes hurried-over as if they were something not quite nice. And when a poet reads his own free verse, I think that I in the audience should hear where his lines end. Also a musical setting should not quarrel with the poet's rhythm, as in the song, "Come into the Garden, Maude".

Our house in Bellevue Road was one of many of that type built in Scottish towns about the turn of the century, well-built of decent-quality stone, and mostly in good order to this day. Each tenement has two main-door houses, with the stair door in between, and the stair in a well right up to the roof, and a big skylight. Ours was the right-hand main-door; there were three flats above, each with three houses. Our old house still shows its number, 109, that my father wrote on the fanlight in gold leaf. He painted many of these houses when they were new, and several of his numbers have survived all those years of window-cleaning.

A few early reminiscences may not come amiss. Don't worry; I have no total recall, but I do remember my surprise on seeing the kitchen table made up as a bed, on which I was laid, and then a sort of bag came down over my nose. That would be when I had my tonsils cut. I remember incidents connected with the Great War. When it began, we were on holiday at Kinghorn, on the other side of the Firth of Forth, which I would think of as the sea. We were going to fight the Germans, who lived on the other side of the sea. The noises were from our own warships. They were all right. Once, when the electric light on our kitchen went dim, that meant that the Zepps were coming, and so they did. My mother was angry with my father for standing at our gate, which was not safe. He was looking at flames in the sky. A whisky warehouse was on fire in Leith. Some people who stayed up the stair saw a Zepp through the big skylight. I got a fright in St Andrew's Square one winter's evening. I thought those big stone figures on the Bank of Scotland were Germans coming over the roof.

The chocolate factory near Portobello (it became the 'Ramsey Tec.' later on) was supposed to have places for German guns on top. Some soldiers in the ward of the 'Fever Hospital', when I was there with diphtheria, taught me a song about "Madamozel from Armiteers". My father was called up by the Army for a medical examination, but we stopped worrying when he came home and said he was C3, or something. He said it was like when his own father, when he couldn't find work, had tried for a job on the building of the Forth Bridge, where a lot of men were killed. My Granny had been pleased when he came back, still idle. My father said *idle*, always, where now we say *unemployed*. I was happy when the Armistice came, but not so happy as I was supposed to be. Then we were all scared about the Flu. To keep it away, my mother bought me a one-inch cube of camphor to wear on a string round my neck, and it worked.

I used to be taken to concerts, and this mention of the Flu reminds me that while that scare was on, I heard Clara Butt in the Central Hall, Tollcross. She sang about a flea and a fly in a flue; I thought it was funny, but the Edinburgh people said such a famous singer should not have sung such a silly song. I remember those words. She sang very distinctly. Much later, I am nearly but not quite sure that I heard Clara Butt, in a celebrity Burns concert in the Usher Hall, singing "Ca' the knowes to the yowes". There were Borderers' Union concerts in the Protestant Institute Rooms, George IV Bridge, and Restoration Fund concerts in the hall of Mill's Kirk, just off Great Junction Street, Leith. All the stonework in the front of that church had to be renewed, and didn't I know it! My father took me to P.S.A. Concerts, (Pleasant Sunday Afternoon) which irked me so much that one day I said I would rather not go: I never suggested such a thing again. He played in the band, and was hurt, though I wondered, at a tender age, how so good a musician could stand so many notes played out of tune. Certain oft-repeated songs produced in me a peculiar bitterness, especially one about a little white bride

48

on her snow-white pillow. In concerts all over Edinburgh and Leith one singer would turn up on the platform several times in one season. She had a strong burr, and yet she would persist in singing "Doon the Burn, Davie Lad". If you recollect how often the word *burn* occurs in the chorus, you will know how awful it sounded. But I did enjoy the recitations and the comic songs, mostly in Scots. Certain songs now pall, but I was amazed and delighted on first hearing "The Wee Cock Sparrie", "The Lum-hat Wantin the Croon" and "Pawkie Paiterson's Auld Grey Yaud". So at least I heard plenty of the Auld Scots Sangs, and as my mother used to say, nothing is wasted in this world. Certainly it was especially exciting to hear the Hawick folk singing "Teribus" at a Borderers' Union concert on the night of the International.

As I remember her, my mother had given up most of her professional playing, but kept on her Saturday afternoon job as 'pianny wumman' at the children's matinées of the 'Picturedrome' near the top of Easter Road. A supermarket now occupies the site of that picture-house that I knew so well. The piano was in a curtained corner to the right of the screen, and there were chairs and stands for the fiddler and cello-player who played in the evening along with another pianist. My mother and I sat in the darkness, with the hooded light of the music-stand and the screen flickering above, or I could look for a seat in the front of the house if I liked. The children got in for a penny each, infants-in-arms for nothing. You would see a boy staggering past the box-office, carrying his wee sister, nearly as big as himself. They read the printed bits of the picture out loud in unison, as if they were in school, and shouted all the time. When the baddie was creeping up behind Pearl White, they all cried "Shoat!", and when she got the better of him, in the last episode of that serial, after I don't know how many Saturdays, they cheered with all their might. But my mother gave them a good pennyworth of music, mostly from memory. Sometimes she put a novel on the stand and read that, while she kept on playing just the same.

Some days my father would take me for walks, I don't mean the formal Sunday walks along familiar streets in our best clothes, when my father would lead the way, three yards in front of my mother and me, until we reached a certain shop where he would buy a paper. Then he would walk along, reading it, three yards behind. The walks my father took me were mystery tours. They could be fun, and we sometimes went on a cable car, which I enjoyed. We might arrive in the yard of some interesting works; there was one where I managed to stand at the foot of a factory chimney, surprised to see how wide it was. But very often our walk would finish on a pavement, with my father disappearing through a doorway while I waited outside. He would be seeing about a job, I daresay. One magic afternoon we went to Granton and he took me on board a ship! It was the paddle-steamer *William Muir*, on which we voyaged the seven miles to Burntisland. For the first time I smelled that magic smell of hot oil and steam and smoke. And you could see the engines. Every few minutes a man threw a bucket of cinders over the side, and I wondered if there was a reef of cinders under the water, all the way. Did that famous ship have only one cylinder, I wonder? I was impressed by the way the whole vessel bent forwards and back with each revolution. One Sunday, with no explanation, my father took me to the Picturedrome. From the front row of the empty hall I watched him set up a high ladder, or maybe a trestle, before the screen, which was a great sheet of moving cloth, with nothing solid behind it. He began to paint the black surround, leaning out of his balance, and getting as much purchase as he dared with one hand on the yielding surface. I could see he was worried. He had only the top to do, and went on painting it from right to left, till after a long time he was finished, and we went home. I knew I had been there to go for help if he had fallen, but nothing was said about that.

I was privileged once to sit in the front row of the Picturedrome balcony, next to Houdini. I even shook hands with him, which took some courage, I can tell you, because we

boys believed that he could squeeze the juice out of a golf-
ball, not a gutty, of course, which was solid cahootchy all
through, but the more up-to-date kind of ball wound with
elastic round a central sphere full of white liquid. The serial
they were showing to that matinée of children was not one of
Pearl White's, for once, but featured Houdini himself. Also
there was a huge Iron Man, and as it slowly balanced from left
foot to right foot the children shouted "Hey! Straw!" "What's
that they're saying?" Houdini asked me. I did my best to
explain, but it took some doing.

I was brought up as a Scottish Episcopalian, maybe
because my mother went "not for the doctrine, but the music
there", and a very good reason, too. Also, I understand, she
was influenced by a churchman named, I assure you, Canon
Ball. I thought I would rather have been a Presbyterian, that
being more Scottish. These thought-processes, by the way,
could work the other way round, as when I reluctantly
decided that I liked the military band in the Gardens better
than the pipe band, because the English had better tunes, I
thought. An embarrassing situation arose when the time came
for me to be confirmed. I was expected to confess my sins. But
I hadn't any. I ran my eye down the list. I had nothing to be
proud about, and did not envy anybody; what would be the
use of that? Anger, no; I had a pretty good temper, and loved
peace better than war. I didn't covet anything either, not
having much chance of getting it anyway. I had recently dug
as much as I could of our allotment. It was full of couch grass,
or *rack*, as we called it. That was a poor bit of ground named
'the Sandies', opposite our house, a disused sand-pit. No, I was
not slothful. Lust, oh no; that was quite out of the question,
and so was Gluttony. The Rector grew impatient. "You don't
mean to tell me you're perfect?" he said. I said no, but
whatever was wrong with me, it was not on the list. Seemingly
only the Seven Deadly Sins would do. I was confirmed just the
same, and have a certificate to prove it, which goes to show
something, but I'm not sure what.

I had forgotten to tell the Rector that I had once been in a celebrated fight, but that was mostly due to the ire of the other boy. I won that fight in very quick time. I landed a beauty right on his nose, and he broke off the engagement, with blood all over his mouth and dripping on his jersey. I did not think he had so much blood in him. And he smeared his hands on his nose all messed up with blood and snot, and it made me so queasy that I fainted! When I came to, he had gone away, leaving a trail behind him.

That took place during a game of one-bat cricket in the Back Field. We had a lot of fun around Bellevue, with many patches of empty ground that still had their ancient names: the Sandies, the Hayfield and Dudgeon's. It would have surprised us if somebody had come and told us he was a play leader and that he was going to show us how to play. We had all sorts of games from one side of the street to the other. If a horse and cart came along, we let it pass. There was a game we called 'Dully', not knowing that *dule* was an ancient Scots word in Jamieson's Dictionary, meaning *goal*. And if we had known, we would have thought nothing of it, because, as I remember well, we spoke with no funny accent or funny words, like people we sometimes met from funny places somewhere else. I was surprised, in fact, that with no merit of my own, I belonged to the top nation and spoke properly.

I will admit that we were not supposed to play football, or to hurl guiders on the pavement, and as wrongdoers we were afraid of the police, who were our friends at other times. Guiders were flat carts or cairties made of boards, that cost fivepence for four wooden wheels, and a bolt and nut to make a pivot for the front axle. The wheels would wear to an oval shape, and catch fire. At the foot of Bellevue Road was a railway siding beyond the soap factory, and we got grease out of the axle-boxes of the trucks, just the thing for guiders.

Speech does persist, especially among children. Right now, I hear them in the street, speaking much as we did, and so do the wee Indians.

52

Opposite our house was the Nursery, and beyond that was Cockie Dudgeon's, where the bus depot is now. The show folk would come there for Christmas, with their caravans and swee-boats and Codona's Golden Dragons and traction engines and steam organs all covered with carving and mirrors and painted figures keeping time to the music. We made friends with the show folk, and after a rainy night we sometimes had free trips on the Helterskelter, as many as we liked, to polish the slides.

Though I wouldn't know, A.D. Mackie stayed, though maybe not just then, in a square beyond Cockie Dudgeon's. His book *Poems in Two Tongues* became a powerful incentive to me in the early thirties.

The language spoken in our house was good Scots, by which I mean that it used many words not found in English, and that it was sounded according to Scottish rules. Reading the recently published *The Guid Scots Tongue*, by David Murison, I realise how grammatically my parents and most of their friends used to speak, according to the rules of Scots. My father had a good schooling from the Episcopalians in return for his services as a choir-boy, but he had to leave early to earn some pay; this made him want to give me as much education as possible. He told me he had been a grocer's boy (closing time 10 p.m., with luck) and had to wet the wine bottles and then sweep the cellar floor to coat them with dust. My mother's schooling began, I think, in Dr Bell's in Leith, and took her as far as the 'Normal School', the training-college for teachers. My mother and some of her friends were members of the Dickens Fellowship, and would talk of his characters as if they were people they knew, which seemed daft to me. I heard their talk when I was in bed for the night in the kitchen bed-recess with a screen across it; I could either listen or fall asleep, an excellent arrangement. I read what I fancied out of the books in the house: Scott, Dickens, a great many novels in red covers, two sets of encyclopedias, a hair-raising pair of books by R.H. Proctor, about planets and comets and

artificial somnambulism and dual consciousness and
mechanical chess players ... I enjoyed scaring myself with
those. I loved R.M. Ballantyne and hated Henty; I borrowed
all sorts of books from the Public Library and read or heard a
good deal of poetry, just as it turned up, Burns's songs
especially, and some of his poems, though the famous poets of
English Literature stood in the big book-case in an expectant
row, like girls at the start of a children's party. I was
encouraged to write verse: birthday greetings and anything
that came along, without thinking anything of it.

Our books mostly came from the Mathewson household. I
have a Burns, for example, with a handsome cover and gilt
edges, of a series named "Moxon's Popular Poets", bought in
the Tolbooth Wynd, and signed "R.H. Mathewson, Leith,
1883". That was my mother's brother Bob, whom she had
liked so much. He was a postman and a popular entertainer in
Leith, which was a small town, independent of Edinburgh,
with a life of its own that makes our kind of society look thin.
The Leith folk all went to his concerts, which brought in
enough money for him to stand an annual treat for the poor
boys of Guthrie's School, I think it would be. My father's
books were mostly about design and decoration; he would tell
me that they had cost a big slice of his pay as a young man. He
had a series of coloured plates of pictures in the National
Gallery. He encouraged me especially to read *The Ragged-
trousered Philanthropists*, which was so true to his own
experience; he, too, had become a decorator, entitled to a
ha'penny an hour above the rate for a brush-hand, and would
find himself finishing a hand-painted frieze on Saturday and
red-leading the bottom of a ship in drydock on Monday. The
painting trade looked a queer mixture to me: there was such a
lot of art in it, colour-schemes and different styles of
decoration, and such a lot of slaistering in dirt and mess, not
of your own making, though the householder would likely
blame you for what was really his own dirt that you were
shifting. The painter comes last of all the tradesmen; he cleans

up everybody's mess and leaves the place ready for people to move in. I did not want to carry on his business. I wanted to be a librarian. I had had enough of helping to push the barrow loaded with planks first, and pairs of steps on top, and pails jammed in between the steps, and things hanging all round, up and down the steep Edinburgh streets; the ups, if anything, being rather easier than the downs. Those were in the early days, certainly; later on my father used to hire a small motor-lorry.

I don't know that my father thought much of me. He was lean and tough, better at moving heavy weights than I have ever been, despite my grandfather, the company porter. That wartime rejection must have been the result of doing the work of two men and a musician on short rations. Whereas I used to be wheezy and asthmatic, subject to terrible coughs and colds, scared of sights like the water splashing far below the open slats of decking at the end of Granton Breakwater, (he was impatient with me over that, and no wonder!) liable to walk right off a plank as I watched what my brush was doing on the ceiling, (that only happened once, I admit) and generally decadent and *fin de siècle* (though he might have used a different expression). What he did was to send me to the gymnasium in Leith Street, run by Charlie Cotter, a friend of his – trainer of champions: Alec Ireland, Tancy Lee – where once a week I was kneaded and embrocated, I swung Indian clubs and biffed three different types of punch-ball, and sparred with George, a thoroughly decent fellow whom I liked immensely, Cotter's young assistant, who knew exactly how to hit, hard but not too hard. What a pity it happened long after my celebrated fight in the Back Field! That was very good for me, no doubt, and so even was my father's contribution to my musical training. I learned to be quite a good accompanist, counting rests and observing pauses. If I missed one, he would shove the scroll of his fiddle in front of my face, counting "Three, four PAUSE". That also would be good for me.

When I was in the Juniors in St James's Episcopal School

near the foot of Broughton Street (still there, but used for some other purpose) my father took advantage of a special offer by the Royal High School, by which he would pay fees of £5 per year that would not be increased during my schooldays. When I left, about ten years later, he considered that he had received good value. So far as I could understand it, the R.H.S. had not been at its best about that time, possibly because of the War, hence the special offer. But it was one of those schools for which Edinburgh was famous but not unique, that did not fail to grind at the wearisome elements of learning (by, with or from a table; oh table!) so we might attain at last to the brainy pleasures of the Sixth Form, a chance of saving your parents' money by coming out high in the Bursary Competition, and a job that would be worth the trouble of getting it. I am not saying that it all worked out perfectly, but that was the general idea. I was privileged at the R.H.S. to be in some pretty brainy company. Professors' sons, for instance, are not all clever, but many of them are, and to measure your ability against theirs is good training and prevents swelling of the head. In that classical school, only the best were deemed good enough to study Greek and Latin. I was not one of these, so I had to take the way of the scientist in the B division. I liked Avogadro's Hypothesis and was impressed by the neatness of Dalton's Atomic Theory, but didn't believe either of them, having got the notion that every theory or hypothesis was something like a fashion, to be superseded after a few years. Such habits of mind were a hindrance to my study of Latin, also; it seemed to be a kind of hypothetical language. How could Caesar make a speech that would satisfy our Latin master, with all the agreements fitting like a jig-saw, just as he was about to throw the Tenth Legion over the river? Also there was no rubbish too stupid for me to attribute to a Latin author when I had to translate his works. But I passed Lower Latin, goal of the B division, and thankfully got on with my volts and ergs and N.T.P.

As for English, it hardly seemed to be a 'subject' at all,

because no rigours were connected with it. I won the Sir Walter Scott Club's Essay Prize: Chambers' *Traditions of Edinburgh*, a book I loved, of which we had a copy at home, but not in such a fine edition; and in the competition for an original poem I came in *proxime accessit* to one of the professors' sons. That prize was a handsomely bound Matthew Arnold, whose poems I couldn't read then, and haven't much enjoyed since. I wish they had given me Robert Fergusson, whom I had not heard of at that time. It would have delighted me to associate his poems with the old Edinburgh buildings that I was getting to know, through reading Chambers' *Traditions* and Grant's *Old and New Edinburgh* which was in our house also. Many of the buildings were described by Grant as "now, alas, swept away", and I thought we would take care not to sweep away any more of those famous houses. But I could see in the twenties how much they were in need of having some money spent upon them. They must have been horrible for the people who stayed in them, and in those days the Canongate and High Street were crammed with people, almost as they were when they fascinated Stevenson. What destruction has happened in half a century since I used to explore those closes with fascination and disgust! The place is a museum; the folk have been mostly moved on and have given place to tourists. I cannot bear to go there any more. But those ancient, life-encrusted buildings influenced me powerfully during my most formative days.

'English' in school was pretty nearly just that in those days; we read much Chaucer but no Barbour, nor any of the Medieval Makars. Gray, Burns and Cowper were lumped together in one literary 'movement'. I suppose the curriculum was linked to the Leaving Certificate and the Bursary Comp. Dr George Davie's book, *The Democratic Intellect*, gives historical reasons. The school was not anti-Scots, and most of the staff were positive in the other direction. Fergusson, however, was a High School boy, and we ought to have been told about him; his plaque, moved from the fine building on the Calton Hill, where it was placed in 1958, now stands at the door of the new Royal High School.

The old building is fine, indeed, and influenced me strongly when I was there. They pulled out the seating of the Hall to re-arrange it for the new Scottish Assembly, and stopped work at that stage. I hope it will be finished soon, and that the Assembly will meet there, and will improve its constitution by its own effort.

In due course, I walked in past the great pillars of the Old Quad, which had filled me with awe long before, when my mother showed them to me, and said I might go there some day. I studied Honours English (we didn't 'read' in those days) and we used to stick our poems on the board of the English Library. Vexed by the englishness of other people's poems, I reacted by presenting "Fi'baw in the Street", glottal stops and all. I thought I was being rude, but it was well received. Mr Murison's *Guid Scots Tongue* tell us how Allan Ramsay's work was one of reaction. I regard mine as a small part of that reaction, which has never quite ceased since Ramsay began it, sometime about 1720.

SELECTED BIBLIOGRAPHY

The Masque of Edinburgh (M. Macdonald 1954); George Buchanan's *Jephthah and the Baptist* Translated in Scots (Oliver and Boyd 1959, now obtainable from Robert Garioch); *Two Men and a Blanket* (Southside 1975); *Collected Poems* (Macdonald Publishers 1977).

4. I Belong to Glasgow

by Maurice Lindsay

Maurice Lindsay is Director of the Scottish Civic Trust. Prior to that he was for many years a well-known broadcaster on TV in Scotland, particularly in connection with arts programmes. He has published twelve volumes of poetry, eleven books of Scottish biography and topography, and a History of Scottish Literature. *He has also edited a number of anthologies.*

There are parts of the world, some not so distant, where to admit that you are a Glaswegian produces either a snigger or a mutter of commiseration. I was born in what is now the Park Conservation Area of the city, and so far have had no cause to regret it. It was, indeed, a desire to reflect the Glasgow experience as I knew it that first impelled me seriously to "commence poet", in Burns's quaint phrase. Where a childhood and adolescence were as happy as mine – the interlude of being morosely unhappy in adolescence, the discovery of the sexual shades, is almost a kind of inverted happiness! – the sights and sounds of early years can hardly fail to stock the imagination. Until I was twenty-one, except for holiday visits to other parts of Scotland and once on a schoolboy trip to France, I never left the country.

The very word *Glasgow* fascinated me. I used to stare at it, separate the syllables and say them aloud. *Glesgie*, it was to some; *Glaschu*, 'the dear green place', to the Gaels who possessed whatever was there, long before the Tobacco Lords built up its Georgian elegance. That was torn down by their Victorian successors in pursuit of expanding profit from their shipyards and factories; profit expended in the magnificent effulgence of public and private building which turned Glasgow into the Second City of the British Empire. A place to be proud to belong to!

Glasgow. A place where you weren't looked at as if you had some repellent disease when you asked what colour of tramcar you should ride on to take you to wherever unfamiliar district you might want to reach! "Warm heart of Scotland with the generous hand", I called it enthusiastically in schoolboy verses, as woefully deficient in a knowledge of anatomy as in the function of imagery.

Glasgow. A virile bustle of change, sheer with life: a fricative edge of social difference; ocean-going ships, nosed high in docks or moored to quays almost at the grey heart of the city; cranes towering like flattened question-marks over the Clyde and the depressed streets of the 'thirties; horse-drawn lorries labouring up hilly West Nile Street; tramcars squealing as they took the corner of Renfield Street and Sauchiehall Street; the stale smell of booze at pub corners; the staler waste of men in dirty white cravats, hanging about the empty day long; the sharp thrust of Glasgow's debased Scots speech, jabbing through elisions and buttressed with sexual oaths. These I remember. And remember, too, the confrontation when, coming home from a Sunday afternoon 'spin' in my father's car, we had to join a long line of waiting cars to let past a banner-carrying procession of hunger-marchers. These were the sights, sounds and smells of a city already sinking into decline, but still mustering enough self-confidence, in what was perhaps by then already non-achievement, to think of itself as 'great'!

I was born into the numerically tiny but then still influential privileged professional sector of this urban interlock of nearly a million people. My father, an insurance manager, was, in his own words, "a self-made man". We were never allowed to forget how much his present position, and therefore ours, depended upon his early sacrifices and unremitting effort. At nineteen, he found himself the eldest of a parentless family of five brothers and sisters. During the last months of the Kaiser's war, part of his left jaw was shot away, and he was pronounced speechless for the rest of his days. A grafted bone from his hip and a technique of rigorously applied courage confounded the doctors. I was almost two years old when he returned from his hospitals to business life. Having inherited nothing from his own father, he brought us up to accept that what he earned – and he was as successful with his investments as with building up the interests of the insurance company whose Scottish office he managed – would be employed in our upbringing and education. Thereafter, we would be on our own. He did not believe in inherited wealth and, until old age, felt that the arts, except for the plays of Shakespeare, were softening and effeminate, but by the time his sight had begun to fail, music had become his main solace. Given a maximum life-expectancy of fifty silent years, he lived to exceed a garrulous eighty-four. Although our relationship was always ambivalent, I admired his courage and his industry.

My mother had a gentler nature. Somewhere along her line there was an opera singer who died young in America. As my mother grew older, my father's constant preoccupation with business, the League of Nations, the Rotary Club and other public causes, together with his lifelong habit of golfing every Saturday with male cronies, isolated her. Although we were a family of four, I came to suspect that there was probably never very much sexual warmth between them. To the disapproval of my father, my mother encouraged my passion for music. When it was clear that I did not mean to be deflected from making a career of it, she slipped me regular sums of money to go to concerts and theatres.

We lived in the West End of Glasgow; at first in the privately-owned Ashton Terrace, parts of which have since been demolished to make way for a road and University buildings, and then in Athole Gardens, an enclosed hilly U-shaped crescent in the high Victorian manner of the 1870s with a private central common garden and a tennis-court. The pink flambeaux of a mature horse-chestnut tree illuminated the front of the house in early summer. From my high-up bedroom window, the roofscape at the back of the house was distantly topped by shipyard cranes.

There was in these days a sense of community about our district of Hillhead. The shopkeepers of Byres Road knew us all by name, and we them. There was Wilkie, the grocer, who sent round a crate of apples at Christmas in appreciation of our custom; the 'thirties equivalent, I suppose, of selling loss-leaders or giving away trading stamps. The three – or was it four? – Misses Horn kept the dairy with the cows at one time in a byre behind the shop, though I cannot recall this. They had hands as blue as the wall-tiles of their shop, due, I used to think, to so much scrubbing. Yet their hands were not as raw as those of the daughter of Andrews, the fishmonger, whose fingers were forever lifting moist fillets off chipped ice. Mr and Mrs Todd, the fruiterers, added their contribution to the Christmas scene with a gift of tangerines to all their 'regulars'. Tully, the ironmonger, and Bell of the toyshop featured less frequently, being on the more occasionally visited periphery of my childish world of things. Most exotic of all was Henderson's stable, from which issued forth the faded, musty-smelling horse-drawn cabs that conveyed us to children's parties. In time, the horses gave place to cumbersome-looking limousines. Cabs and limousines have been swept away for a supermarket, where well-wrapped things wait on their shelves without that warmth of human contact the older way of shopping provided. Yet I still have a childish liking for shopping, a liking celebrated in my poem "How Do You Do?"

MAURICE LINDSAY

During the absence of my father in hospital, a bachelor uncle of my mother's – John by name, though my childish lips could get no nearer to it than Doan, which he always remained – acted as a much-loved substitute, a role he maintained until his own brief marriage late in life. A grain merchant, he kept his samples in heavy manilla envelopes from which he extracted the pulses on broad ivory samplers to show to shopkeepers. I enjoyed watching him check their freshness before each new week began.

Every Saturday, he would take me on an excursion. It might involve jolting the length of a tuppenny tram-ride to some distant and magically-named suburb such as Auchenshuggle; or sailing model yachts or steamboats, bought by him, on the pond in Victoria Park. Once, it was an illicit journey on a real tanker steam-engine from Hyndland depot. My uncle got a row from my mother when we arrived home furtively with tell-tale oil marks on my Sunday jacket.

Sometimes our excursions carried us far outside Glasgow. When I was about eight or nine, we took a bus ride into Lanarkshire. Suddenly, the bus was surrounded by shouting men who made us all get out. Sweating and swearing, they pushed the bus over on its side. For many months after, the long tinkle of falling glass which followed the crash as the bus rolled over, sounded through nightmares in which I was leered at by the contorted faces of the protesting miners, sweating to dislodge a bus's equilibrium. I did not understand how pushing over a bus could help to get anyone jobs. Doubtless an adult hatred of, and contempt for, violent protest movements and Trade Union bullying, were established on that long-ago Saturday afternoon.

As I grew up, I became increasingly aware of the dichotomies between which our way of life was balanced: affluence against poverty, a nominal Protestantism against Jewery and Catholicism. My father frequently reminded us of our good fortune, urging us to "Count our blessings, count them one by one". My mother and her friends, and even our

63

three domestics, often let fall sharp comments about Catholics and the Jews. This puzzled me. The nanny employed to look after my younger brother and sisters seemed the mostly likely source of information. The Jews, she explained, killed Christ, and were too fond of making money. No greater accusation against the Catholics was levelled than that they were 'left footers'. For some time after, I used surreptitiously to examine the walk of a Catholic schoolmaster to see how this peculiarity affected him.

The most obvious dichotomy, of course, was between those who were more or less well off, like ourselves, and those who decidedly were not. My father's Calvinistic insistence on the reward-earning virtues of hard work was scarcely the whole answer, as he himself admitted. On the way into town with my mother for tea in Copland and Lye's – then a store with an elegant tier of galleries, afterwards filled in to provide more floor-space – our yellow tram often passed knots of aimless men hanging about the shabbier corners of Dumbarton Road. The tinkling restaurant music of the John MacArthur Quintet counterpointing the chinking of dishes and trays, and the gossip of my mother's friends set me wondering, in early 'teens about:

> the comfortable forgetfulness of the many
> who lie in content's soft arms, and are safe and sure
> in the fabled Grecian wanderer's lotus-land:
> who forget the sullen glove of the wet grey skies,
> and the lashing Northern wind that flicks the skin,
> where hum-drum poverty's dull and listless eyes
> are pressed to the window, hearing the friendly din
> of the party, watching the lights and laughter within.

> But oh! I cannot forget. So I wait and wonder:
> how long will the thinly-dividing window hold?
> how long will the dancing drown the terrible anger
> of those, the unwanted, who peddle their grief in the cold,
> wrapped in their own despair's thick and unkindly fold?

From an early age I had been subjected to a personal discipline which I hated at the time, but which was undoubtedly to prove valuable, even if perhaps it also laid the grounds of adult cynicism. Respect for the truth, my father called it, insisting that the truth always wore three aspects: my version, the other man's, and the story somewhere in between. This third view, the "real" truth as he called it, often never seemed to appear until, as I discovered later Coventry Patmore so neatly put it, "none cares whether it prevails or not". When other children were playing in the summer sun, I used to have to apply this truth test to daily holiday exercises that my father devised to develop memory and concentration. One such exercise was copying out and memorising a poem a day. I soon realised that the speeches of politicians, also used as exercise source material, could rarely be accepted as representing my father's idea of "real" truth. I began to develop a wary sense of non-involvement with surface truth strengthened by my growing fascination with music and literature, which seemed to state unchallengeable truths. These things, I speculated, must exist outside, *there*, in their own right. Obviously, a poem by Shelley, or a symphony by Mozart, had a continuing relevance and 'reality' denied to the popular songs on the wireless, like:

> Around the corner, under the tree,
> The gallant major made love to me.

or:

> The King's horses, the King's men,
> They rode up the street and they rode back again.

Doubtless military men did make love and the cavalry did indulge in pointless equestrian manoeuvres. Not until many years later, when I encountered the World 3 theory of Sir Karl Popper, did I find a satisfactory philosophical explanation for this puzzling phenomenon.

Paradoxically, this growing feeling of non-involvement with

dogmas and absolutes led me, years later, to become, among other things, a radio and television interviewer and reporter, stimulating my curiosity about other people. For as long as I can remember I have had an insatiable interest in the mechanics of other people's lives: their jobs, enthusiasms, prejudices and opinions. Once, on holiday at Prestwick, I subjected two little boys who were holidaying in the house across the road to such a detailed cross-examination about their parents, who happened to belong to an unusual religious sect, that I was suspected of having been "put up" to it, and an indignant protest was lodged with my father. But I grew up convinced that extreme views or solutions were rarely likely to be correct; that the truth, if discernible at all, was most likely to be found somewhere between the zigs and zags of polarities; and that the ultimate 'solutions' provided by Christ – or, at least, the Church – and Marx were certain to be false. Marx, with whom I tangled much later, has no place here; but religion, ritually enforced by non-believing parents on their defenceless young, has.

My religious disillusion had something to do with that cruel moment when the reindeer-driving gift-bringing image of Santa Claus – he who so miraculously changed shape to negotiate snow-pitched roof and sooty chimney – lay, a crumpled heap on my parents' bedroom floor. If you could not trust a miracle attested to by your parents, in what sort of substantiated wonder could you believe? (It took me years to realise that the great thing about wonder is its essentially unsubstantiality!)

My mother never showed any interest in religion. My father was nominally a member of Trinity Church, Claremont Street, now the rehearsal hall of the Scottish National Orchestra. Although a clarion faith had evidently blazed from its pulpit in the days of the Reverend Dr John Hunter, the incumbent by this time was an actor manqué, the Reverend H.S. Maclelland, whose doctrines appeared to embrace all shades of religious belief, and none. Even to-day, non-church-going parents in Scotland still like their children to be inculcated at school with religious beliefs they themselves have consciously rejected. Presumably my agnostical father – who, almost on his death-bed, dismissed the Christian belief in an after-life as "absurd damned nonsense" – felt that I would benefit in some way by exposure to Church of Scotland orthodoxy.

So I was sent, first, to Sunday School, of which all I can recollect is a sensation of hard-seated boredom, and then to Hillhead Parish Church, a great oval of hanging space built in imitation of the Sainte Chapelle in Paris. There, I listened weekly to the sermons of the Reverend Dr W.D. Maxwell, a Scoto-Catholic who wore different-coloured vestments in accordance with the seasons of the Christian year. Dr Maxwell, who eventually occupied a Chair of Divinity in a South African University, preached ethics, for the most part, to a congregation of elderly spinsters, relics of once-wealthy West End business families, professional bachelors who 'did' for themselves, and a few middle-aged couples. I enjoyed the ethics, but apparently the rest of the congregation did not. Increasingly, they stayed away. So Dr Maxwell turned to dogma. The bleeding lamb imagery of the butcher's shop revolted me (as also, I discovered later, it once did Shaw). The thought that millions upon millions of dreary, bored Christian people might have to endure each other in some sort of crowded celestial presence for an eternity beyond all conception of time, absolutely horrified me. I felt sorry for God, if this was really what He had let himself in for, though I did not, on the whole, think it likely. Even after I became convinced that the Christian religion, as formalised by the various rival Churches, was basically derived from a monk-made structure, devised by man and not by God, I kept on going to church, because the organ, the gift of a famous whisky family, filled the hanging space with the argument of Bach and Mendelssohn, the vibrating rhetoric of Widor, Karg-Elert and Rheinberger.

Music was now becoming an obsession with me. From the age of twelve, when I abandoned the piano as my main instrument in favour of the violin, I wanted to earn my living as a musician, preferably as a composer able to pour out ordered enchantment like Haydn! A broadcast of his "Military" symphony, heard as I lay on the hearth-rug of family friends with the courtesy titles of aunt and uncle, at their home in Courthill, Bearsden, made me shiver physically with inexplicable delight. Although I did attempt to follow this ambition to become a composer, I soon discovered that words rather than notes came more naturally to my pen. Nevertheless, I still wanted to be a violinist.

My first teacher, Elsie Maclaurin, was a descendant of Colin Maclaurin, the great mathematician of Edinburgh's eighteenth-century Enlightenment. An etching of the famous man hung on the wall of her music-room in Glasgow Street, Hillhead. The similarity of their features, especially the noses separated by two hundred years, was uncanny. Apart from routine lessons, Elsie Maclaurin organised quartet parties and other gatherings, and great was the civilising pleasure these happy informal evenings in her wise company gave me.

In due course she felt that I needed more advanced teaching, and passed me on to Camillo Ritter, an immigrant Austrian from Graz. Something of a recluse, he had studied with Joachim and Sevcik, and played the Brahms Violin Concerto in the presence of the composer. Though a strict upholder of classicism in violin-playing, spiritually he was immersed in the German Romanticism of his boyhood, and with this powerfully he affected me. Slight and white-haired, with jaw that thrust out a further inch at the merest suggestion of a technical difficulty being insuperable, most of his fellow musicians in Glasgow thought him in some way an eccentric failure; perhaps because he had not amassed for himself a fortune, like his many-secretaried cousin, the composer of "White Horse Inn". When my father, exasperated by my determination to persist in concentrating on becoming a violinist rather than training for the safer occupation of a teacher of music in schools, eventually declared that he would no longer pay for my lessons and that I must go into business without further delay, Ritter continued to teach me for nothing.

Other circumstances intervened to deflect me from the career I so much desired. While I was exercising a dog on a disused coal bing near Bearsden, the animal appeared to lose its grip. Reaching out to save it, I lost my own footing, and in the ensuing fall injured a small bone in the wrist of my bowing-arm; damage that a subsequent war injury increased. Also, I fell in love for a second time. Although my beloved was herself a musician, she sided with my father over the teaching business (though nothing else), and my determination was attacked from a vulnerable angle. Then came Munich, when the shadow that had attached itself to my generation lengthened ahead of us and was at last seen to be filled with substance.

A year later, my time ceased to be my own. Music was clearly not compatible with the duties of a second lieutenant in the Army, and my girl married another. The loss of her hurt. It was eventually exorcised in the poem "London, September 1940".

My third-time-lucky falling-in-love, which has led to more than thirty years of happy marriage, lies outside the scope of these pages; unlike my first, which smote me at the beginning of my serious school-days. Pat was of ages with me, both of us twelve. Tall, skinny, with chuckling eyes and a mop of frizzy hair, she met me every day at the corner of Byres Road and Great George Street. There, we spent over an hour a day exchanging tender nothings. She 'inspired' my first published verses, a declaration of love from Damon to Sylvia. They appeared in the school magazine and attracted the attention of the Latin master, 'Foxy' Clark, a dominie of the old school who glinted through gold-rimmed spectacles over a peaked starched collar. "Lindsay's poem", though in English, was given out as the night's homework. Next day, I was called in front of the class to repeat what I had learned. "You have made three mistakes," growled 'Foxy'. "Hold out your hand." "But sir," I protested, "I was reciting the revised version." "Your task was to learn the prescribed text. Hold out your hand." There may be some who think that the beating which followed cannot have been hard enough.

My public school-days at the Glasgow Academy were, on the whole, less important to me than my private musical upbringing; except for the arrival in my life – or, more accurately, my arrival in the class – of B.G. Aston, an English teacher known affectionately as 'Baggy' because of the cut of his flannel trousers and his rolling nautical gait. 'Baggy', (who turned out to be a Territorial soldier, not a sailor) made literature live by communicating a quality of enthusiasm not normally associated by pupils with schoolmasters. Not that he was in any sense an actor. When he declaimed Shakespeare, he fell back upon the intrusive *huh*:

"Is this a dagger – *huh* – that I see before me –
Huh – the handle towards my hand?"

or:

"I know a bank – *huh* – whereon the wild thyme grows".

Yet the *huhing* did not matter. He knew, and brought his pupils to know, that the true end of poetry is delight. Admittedly, he once described Burns as "a minor song-writer you can read in your own time", and led us to believe that poetry died in Greece with Rupert Brooke. Thus ill-armed, eventually I had to flounder through the morass of the New Apocalypse and the linguistic over-assertiveness that animated the Lallans Makars before I learned how to be about what I really wanted to do. All the same, my debt to 'Baggy' was, and is, a huge one.

Glasgow Academy has produced many distinguished soldiers, statesmen, doctors, businessmen, and, of course, Sir

James Matthew Barrie O.M., whose brother still taught French in the school while I was there. Its curriculum, like that of other public schools, was then still designed to produce 'leaders', and was ill-equipped to cater for the needs of a musico-literary eccentric. I was the first student to take music as a subject at Higher Leaving Certificate level, my oral examiner being the composer Francis George Scott, on whom I inflicted the test piece, Raff's *Cavatina*. The classics were encouraged and, even more so, the pursuits of rugby and the Officer's Training Corps. The military lore I gained reluctantly from this organisation probably stood me in good stead, as things turned out. The weakness of the school was that if you were disinclined to work at uncongenial subjects, no one made sure you did. Its strengths were the breadth of opportunity it offered and the unobtrusive manner in which it inculcated self-reliance and self-discipline, qualities glibly denigrated today, but even more essential to artists than to others.

Holidays in the country were mainly an enrichment of the faculty of discovery. For many years we had spent part of each summer in the Highlands for the benefit of my father, a keen fisher, and part at Prestwick for the benefit of his sand-loving family. One day my father announced a change of plan. We were going to 'The Coast'. He and my mother disappeared for a day and came back with the news that they had rented a house for the whole two months of the summer holidays at Innellan, on the Clyde.

Repeated furtive last minute checks to make sure that tickets, passport, foreign currency, or whatever, have not been forgotten, becomes a phobia. I sometimes wonder if my anxiety to be sure that nothing essential for a journey has been left behind had its origins in the ritualistic preparations gone through annually before the Lindsay family left Athole Gardens for the Broomielaw to board the splendid and venerable paddle-steamer *Columba* for the three-hour sail "doon the watter" to Innellan. In these days bed linen had to be transported, as well as suitable clothing for all possible variants of Clyde Coast weather during the months of July and August. An assortment of battered saratoga trunks, fully packed, was assembled in the hall the night before departure, because the horse-drawn lorry to convey the luggage to the steamer – which cast off at precisely eleven minutes past seven – arrived at five-thirty in the morning. Well in advance, everyone was allotted his or her task for the final hours. The most onerous duty was to ensure that Laddie, the cat, kept unbasketed until the last possible moment, did not escape when the front door was wedged open while the carters were lugging out the heavy trunks on their backs.

The sail itself, past shipyards alive with noisy riveting and metallic clanging, was an experience as unforgettable as it is to-day unrepeatable. I have described it in my prose tribute to my native city, *Portrait of Glasgow*.

Tucked beneath the Cowal hills and facing across the estuary towards Largs and the seaward arms of the Firth, Innellan was in those days a child's paradise. Corraith, the house my parents had rented, had been built in the 1870s by a Glasgow tea-merchant, James Pringle, as a holiday home. (He is the subject of my poem "Corraith, Innellan".) It stood at the top of a long strip of flower-lined lawn. Through ornamental gates, the front garden reached down almost to the sea, the road between a kind of invisible ha-ha, except when traffic passed. The equally long garden behind, terraced with fruit and vegetables, rose steeply towards the back road, crowned by the U.F. church. Pleasure-steamers crossed and re-crossed the tracery of that gate many times an hour. Creeping along the opposite coast, the Irish packets kept their more distant morning and evening passages. Every now and then, especially at week-ends, liners from Canada and America glided majestically in and out again, having set down or picked up passengers at the Tail of the Bank, off Greenock. Less exalted craft fussed continuously about their smaller occasions. There was scarcely a moment of the day or night when the waters of the Firth were not animated by the movement of a vessel.

To begin with, in the early days, there was the sound and 'feel' and smell of the shore. Fifty years on, I revisited it. Little had changed:

Sheltered behind a rock a woman sits
keeping an eye on more than what she knits;
her hands the flashing motion of the sea,
veined with the dulse of vulnerability.

The same reflected sky, the same blue shout
through which a bather plunges, and runs out,
his sticky skin rubbed dry with towelled grit,
a gravelly biscuit for his chittering bit.
Though different the clothes, the cut of ships,
the waves still curl those same contemptuous lips
that split the wrack of winter up the beach
like purposes unshaped from human reach.

Gulls, stiff as saddles, ride the little bay
much as they rode the winds of yesterday.
A toy yacht arrows over shallow water
wafted by splashing knees and yells of laughter.
The boy beside the pool lets down his hand
to guddle baby crabs from shifting sand.

Watching alone, an old man nobody knows,
catching inquiring looks, gets up and goes.

The garden was fringed by two continuous herbaceous plots running from the sides of the house towards the gate. The summer was filled with colour and scent, a seemingly random profusion of roses, tiger-lilies, hydrangeas, phlox, carnations and catmint. Monkey-puzzles and palms grew stuntedly in the temperate sea air. Up the hilly back garden, a path led through an overgrown gate to the hill road, which gradually narrowed to a path that led to the grass-covered ruins of an early clachan.

Like most of the Clyde Coast resorts, Innellan was developed from a Gaelic-speaking hamlet into a holiday extension of Glasgow. The merchant princes of the nineteenth century took advantage of the coming of the steamboat, making travel reliable and regular, to build themselves summer villas in a profusion of borrowed styles. In the face of this determined urban onslaught, the ancient Gaelic culture retreated northwards, over those Cowal hills that had once been a frontier between Highlands and Lowlands. In the 'thirties, some families still owned houses built by their prosperous ancestors. Others were already in the hands of people who supplemented their income in retirement by 'letting' to Glasgow families. Few had then been divided into flats.

Many of my early poems derive directly from the Innellan experience. Much more stored itself away in my subconscious. That experience still sometimes surprises me by presenting its imagery when called forth by some parallel not always on the surface apparent. My affection for the place was so strong that round it I wove a kind of personal mythology:

A wet-nosed morning snuffles around the door,
fawning upon me not to go away;
and I, as if I'd never gone before,
    feel half impelled to stay;

as I intercept the sun's awakening scrawl
on the village doused beneath a browsing hill;
and I hear the stretch of the waves as they yawn and
    sprawl,
    smiling their aimless fill.

The morning milk-cart jolts its jangling load,
dripping a spitter of stars beside shut gates,
its bored horse pawing sparks from the metalled road
    as he trots, and stops and waits.

The red-cheeked postman's out on his cycle rounds,
ferrying news from beyond, through bordered flowers
and, rising from roadside verges, the echoing sounds
    of yesterday's sunny hours.

Don't go, the familiar signals whisper, tempt me;
forget what's to do and succumb to the sense of Now,
where time's unhurried turning breathes Forever,
    only the heart knows how.

Half of me feels these blood-heard urges are right;
that I'll miss one trailing wheel of a Cowal sun,
burning its layer of coloured change by to-night,
    when the news and the milk are done.

Then I think of the way of the world, the buying and
    selling
that knits it together; how everything's shaped by the
    mind,
whose insistent inner voice keeps silently calling:
    you daren't get left behind.

The fluttering thump of the fussing paddle-steamer
slows as it sizzles and sidles into the pier.
Hurry, the gangway clatters: *for schemer or dreamer*
    there's no such place as Here.

People and places are the themes of most of my poetry. I
count myself lucky to have been able to assimilate through the
quick pulse of youth the 'feel' of Glasgow and the loveliness of
the Firth of Clyde before they both entered upon shabby
decline. During the decade or so before September 1939,
Innellan looked out upon a prospect of sea and hills as
spectacular as anything in Europe. Now, the big ships have
gone, their purpose supplanted by aircraft. The friendly
paddle-steamers and turbines, named after characters in the
Waverley novels, gods of the ancient World and Scottish
duchesses, have been banished to the breaker's yard by the

omnipotence of the motor-car. The complete failure of our post Second World War planning to preserve an officially acknowledged area of outstanding scenic beauty has resulted in the siting of a hideous electricity generating station at Inverkip (instead of at Dundonald, in Ayrshire, where its assertiveness might even have been an asset on a bleak stretch of coast), its chimney groping above the line of the hills, opposite Dunoon. An economically unnecessary steel port surrounds Hunterston. A massive site for the construction of concrete North Sea oil platforms has violated the mouth of Loch Striven and the entrance to the Kyles of Bute. Only two platforms have been built in it, and already it has ceased to serve its environmentally destructive function.

Glasgow has fared little better. Facing a contracting future, it struggles to adapt to some as yet undiscovered new purpose, facilities that related to industrial and economic circumstances that are never likely to return again.

No one wants to go back to his childhood, however happy or imaginatively fruitful it may have been. Few writers rely wholly on autobiographical promptings. For me, indeed, a poem can as easily rise out of a phrase in a newspaper or an overheard conversation. The memory of an arresting face can send me off along the track of fancied biography. People as well as places have been equally my 'subjects'.

Nevertheless, the recollections of childhood and adolescence do provide a kind of private buttress. Change has become so rapid and far-reaching that many people seem to feel the psychological need for some sort of evidence of continuity. In the daily world about us, the conservation of the best of our man-made heritage, townscape and cityscape helps to provide some necessary physical reassurance. Perhaps a vivid recollection of the days that are gone can lend us at least a perspective of the spirit in a technologically-orientated age, when the pursuit of poetry sometimes appears to be a pastime scarcely less futile than talking to oneself.

MAURICE LINDSAY

SELECTED BIBLIOGRAPHY

Walking Without An Overcoat: Poems 1972–76 (1977); *History of Scottish Literature* (1977); *Selected Poems: 1942–72* (1973); *Portrait of Glasgow* (1972); *The Burns Encyclopedia* (1959, Rev. 1970); *The Lowlands of Scotland – Edinburgh and the South* (1956, Rev. 1976); *Robert Burns: The Man; His Work; The Legend* (1954, Rev. 1969); *The Lowlands of Scotland – Glasgow and the North* (1953, Rev. 1973).

5. My Way of It

by *Norman MacCaig*

Norman MacCaig was born in Edinburgh in November 1910 and educated at the Royal High School and Edinburgh University, where he took an honours degree in Classics. He was a schoolteacher from 1934 to 1967, and Headmaster from 1969 to 70 and was Fellow in Creative Writing at Edinburgh University from 1967 to 1969. Since 1972 he has been Reader in Poetry at the University of Stirling. He was given the Heinemann Award in 1967 and is a Fellow of the Royal Society of Literature. With Alexander Scott, he edited Contemporary Scottish Verse 1959–1969. *A keen fisher, he spends part of each summer in Sutherland.*

A PREFATORY EXCHANGE

> 7 Milton Hill,
> Milton,
> Dumbarton.
> 17 August 1977

Dear Norman,

I wonder if you would like to contribute an essay of about five thousand words on the influences of your childhood and adolescence on your poetry for an anthology I am editing, *A I Remember* ... an extension of your *Chapman* article?

Since quite a number of our contemporaries and colleagues will be of the company, the book should make up a useful and interesting collection, and I hope you will agree to be one of our number.

> Yours aye,
>
> Maurice

> 7 Leamington Terrace,
> Edinburgh.
> 23 August 1977

Dear Maurice,

I have a hundred horsepower revulsion from writing about myself – the *Chapman* article you mention is the nearest I got to it – and so I am sorry but I don't want to contribute to your book which, on the other hand, I'll read with interest.

I *am* sorry, but it's just not in my nature.

> Norman

> 1 April, 1978

Dear Norman,

There is nothing significant about the date of my coming back to you on the question of a contribution for the anthology *As I Remember*. Of the ten writers who agreed to contribute, nine have sent in their essays. The tenth, Edwin Morgan, after having made several attempts at his, has told me on the telephone that nothing much that happened to him before the age of forty now interests him. He asks to be relieved of his contract. Naturally though with a feeling of disappointment on behalf of future readers, I have agreed.

This leaves a hole in my book. Your *Chapman* contribution

was so good that I hope I can now persuade you to allow us reprint it with due acknowledgement to the Editor.

As aye,

Maurice

8 April, 1978

Dear Maurice,

I've taken so long to write to you because I couldn't find the appropriate *Chapman*. I just got my grips on it this morning ...

Best wishes,

Norman

MY WAY OF IT

A man, whether he likes it or not, can't climb down from his genealogical tree and scramble up another of his own choice. To go back, then, only two generations, three of my grandparents were Gaels and the fourth was a Border Scot from Dumfriesshire. She's the one who gets me to places on time.

I am, that's to say, a threequarter Gael. Now, Celtic art is not at all the romantic, not to say sentimental thing of popular belief. Its extreme formality is to be seen in all the forms it takes – in its carvings and sculptures, its personal ornaments, its poetry and its music. (Think of pibroch.) All those genes I carry about, therefore, incline me strongly towards the classical rather than the romantic, the Apollonian rather than the Dionysian, and this inclination was both revealed and supported by the fact that I took a degree in Classics. By some, sloped in the other direction, my work has at times been criticised as being, to their taste, too cool, too restrained, too controlled. Naturally, this doesn't bother me at all. My defence, if I were to make one, would be restrained murmurings about the disinction between passion and emotion and a smug re-telling of Mallarmé's answer to the lady who asked him, "Do you not, then, ever weep in your poetry, Mons. Mallarmé?" "No, madame," he said, "and I don't blow my nose in it either."

This means, too, that I have always had a great and to some degree an exploratory interest in prosody and rhymes. Until about ten years ago, or less, I wrote only in stanzas that were metrical and used rhymes. But I was aware of the bullying authority of the compulsively iambic nature of English and particularly of the danger of adding to the thousand miles of banal iambic pentameters. But my way of "breaking the neck of the iambic" was not, for many years, the Poundian one of flopping into free verse and deserting the basic element of the metrical foot in favour of the looser, and more variable (and more difficult) basis of the cadence, or phrase. I tried to rescue my metrical lines from a rocking-horse humpty-dumpty by using off-beat stresses – but not so off-beat that the ghostly paradigm of the iambic pentameter (for instance) was not to be noticed behind the frailer metrics I was using. I also began to indulge more and more the ancient practice, publicised as "sprung rhythm" and often overdone by Gerald Manley Hopkins, of taking liberties with the number of syllables in the foot – but, again, still preserving the fundamental iambic movement of the line.

In much the same way, I very soon became bamboozled by the apparent assumption of many people that the only rhymes were those in which the final vowel, or vowels, and the final consonant happily chimed in consort (sin, begin: sorrow, tomorrow: Proteus, hello tae us) and I was soon writing what many people would say weren't rhymes (road, red: mud, fur: full, pale: backs, taxi). I say "then", because this sort of thing has now become common enough practice. All this was nothing new, of course. Gaelic poetry has been assonantal for centuries and I believe Irish Gaelic poetry exploited about every kind of rhyme you haven't thought of. At any rate, anyone interested in such fascinating delicacies need look no further than the Irish English verses of that insufficiently recognised poet, Austin Clarke.

There came an evening, however, eight or nine years ago, when I broodily sat down to write a poem and to my surprise the little thing was fledged in free verse. I of course produced more of the same and got very interested in the techniques of this, to me, new form. Whoever it was – was it Graves, or Auden? – who said, in contempt of free verse, that it was like playing tennis without a net, was talking through a hole in his own practice. The formal structure of a metrical, rhymed poem may be in some respects a restricting straitjacket, but it also keeps you from flailing your arms about in meaningless, shapeless gestures, and it's my belief that to write a formally good poem in free verse is more difficult than to mosaic away with iambs and feminine rhymes.

How many free verse poems are ruined by the lack of a through-going rhythm to articulate the whole and by line-endings which are purely arbitrary and serve no functional purpose whatever.

The thing is, art, whatever else it may be or do, is concerned with form, and that's to say, with order. I don't know whether artists see an order in the chaos of experience that other people don't or whether they impose an order on that chaos. But that order must be there. To defend formless and chaotic writing on ground that it's an enactment of the chaotic times we live in is to committ that aesthetic sin, the fallacy of imitative form, and to renege from the primary duty of any artist, in whatever mode he is operating.

I also hatefully reject the limiting notion, bannered and free-floated most spectacularly by A. Alvarez, that, the times being what they are, the only poetry possible is a poetry of extremes, scribbled frantically on your way back from a mental hospital to commit suicide. Of course there is poetry to be written from the far edge of consciousness, of suffering, of despair. But into my, and your, five ports of knowledge come many cargoes and we should unship the lot. If art is to be concerned only with the tragic or, even, only with the huge concepts of death, alienation, love, loss of Eden, and what the devil is Time anyway, a vast amount of the great art of the past will have to be rejected as 'irrelevant'. There's conceit for you. I also detest the notion that *all* art is a therapeutic expression of inner, psychological tensions, of the quarrel with ourselves whose expression Yeats thought produces poetry as opposed to rhetoric. Of course that is true of a great deal of art. But what about the other great deal, whose cause, purpose and effect is pure celebration of a woman or a chair or a landscape? Are we to dismiss these as trivial? If so, I have written a good many trivial poems, and here's one.

Ringed Plover by a Water's Edge

They spring eight feet and
stop. Like that. They
sprintayard (like that) and
stop.
They have no acceleration
and no brakes.
Top speed's their only one.

They're alive – put life
through a burning-glass, they're
its focus – but they share
the world of delicate clockwork.

In spasmodic
Indian file
they parallel the parallel ripples.

When they stop
they, suddenly, are
gravel.

In my self-belittling way I call poems of this kind (they're really celebratory) 'snapshot poems', a bad habit I keep meaning to break.

I said poetry involves order. It has to submit to the control of the rational mind – it's not enough to lift the trap-door to the subconscious and lasso whatever crawls out. I say this, blushing with guilt, for there was a time in the thirties and early forties when that is pretty much what I did. Poem after poem was a splurge of hardly related images, sloppily bound together – and it wasn't enough – only by the blessed formalities of metre and rhyme. An odd thing is that men from Cornwall to Edinburgh (and Glasgow), who didn't know each other or what the others were up to, found themselves writing in this same, foolish way. They became known as the New Apocalypse and serve them right. I was rescued by the only critical remark that was ever any use to me, when my second book came out and a friend, having read it, handed it back to me, saying, "When are you publishing the answers?" This took me several steps back towards my senses and I started on the long haul towards lucidity. Some years later I read, in a novel by Peter de Vries, a nice remark made by a woman to her husband about a friend of theirs: "He's profound on the surface but deep down he's shallow," and I greeted that with a fanfare. The label "Apocalyptic" stuck, as labels do, long after it was contravening the Trades Descriptions Act and even yet I occasionally hear it and am reduced to shuddering fits and grittings of teeth, for it's long since I decided that poems which are wantonly or carelessly obscure (not difficult) are bad art and bad manners.

I don't remember being unusually interested in poetry at school (perhaps because so much of what we were given was romantic?), but what started me off occurred there. When I was in the fifth form at the Royal High School, the English teacher, Puggy Grant (a nice man) said that by next Wednesday we were to write an essay on something or other, or a poem. Well, I thought, a poem is shorter. So I wrote a poem – to the tune, interestingly enough to those who know me, of a Gaelic song, which I would name if I could spell it. It was, naturally, awful.

From then on I wrote a tremendous number of 'poems' of an elaborate and increasing awfulness that culminated in the Apocalyptic riddlemerees I mentioned above. I think one reason for this was that it never entered my head to try to get them published. Since I had no audience, the fact that they were incomprehensible seemed to matter little. My friend's remark, however, jolted me with the realisation that a poem is a form of communication, and what can you communicate in gobbledygook?

All the same, my writing habits haven't changed much. When I feel like writing a poem, I sit down with a blank sheet of paper and no idea whatever in my head. Into it, where there's plenty of room, enters the memory of a place, an emotional experience, a person, or, most commonly, a phrase, and the poem stalactites down the page from that. This means I'm into the poem, various distances, before I know what it's about. In fact I don't know what the whole poem's about till I've finished it. This sounds daft, but I believe it's a common enough experience with poets.

Sometimes, even, I think I've written a poem on theme A and when I read it I find I've written a poem on theme B or, more commonly, theme A + B – as, for example in this one

Birthdays
In the earliest light of a long day
three stags stepped out from the birch wood
at Achmelvich bridge
to graze on the sweet grass
by the burn.
A gentle apparition.

Stone by stone a dam was built,
a small dam, small stone by stone.

And the water backed up, flooding
that small field.

I'll never see it again.
It's drowned for ever.
But still
in the latest light of a lucky day I see
horned heads come from the thickets
and three gentle beasts innocently pacing
by that implacable water.

While writing this, I took it to be a 'snapshot poem' only, and it was nearly finished before I realised that it was not only a description of that place and those events, it was also about time and memory. It could be, I think, that each stone in the dam is a year of my life (hence the title) and the water is time, drowning what was known and now exists only in the memory.

Many poets polish and refine and eliminate and add, making version after version of the original attempt. I can't do that. The poem, whatever its worth, generally comes easily and quickly and pretty often with no correction at all, and once it's on the page, that's that. This hit or miss way of writing means that I write a lot. It also means I write a lot of unimprovable duds. I reckon at least half, probably more, of what I write I put in the bucket – an act I relish almost as much as writing the things. It's a wasteful form of production which I recommend to nobody.

My notions about the value of poetry and the ways it is produced are, I've come to notice, fairly low-falutin'. I never met a White Goddess in my life and when I find myself in the company of singing robes, hieratic gestures and fluting voices I phone a taxi. The pleasure in making poems lies in making them and seems to me not different from a true craftsman's pleasure in making a table, or a meal to put on it, or a boat that marries the water as a boat should. The pleasure in making something that was never in the world before, with our gifts and abilities at their farthest stretch, is surely one that is common to everybody.

I'm not, of course, denying the special, unique and practical importance of poetry and the other arts. The nub and centre (pith, if you like) of my thinking about that is this: An adult physique with the intelligence of a child is looked after as potentially dangerous. But an adult intelligence along with the emotional equipment of a child is even more so. Intellect and sensibility – the arts develop both. Poetry teaches a man to do more than observe merely factual errors and measurable truths. It trains him to have a shrewd nose for the fake, the inflated, the imprecise and the dishonest. So, it compels him to resist stock responses, because it compels him to examine the emotional significance, as well as the rational significance, of whatever comes under his notice. To have unexamined emotional responses is as immature, as dangerous, as to have unexamined beliefs. And what proportion, I wonder, of the misunderstandings and miseries in the world are due to no more than the stock use of big words – liberty, patriotism, democracy and all their dreary clan – and the stock response to them?

SELECTED BIBLIOGRAPHY

Old Maps and New (1978); *Tree of Strings* (1977); *The World's Room* (1974); *The White Bird* (1973).

6. Growing Up with Granite

by *Alexander Scott*

Alexander Scott was born in Aberdeen in 1920, the son of a power-loom tuner, and was educated there and in the army, where he saw action as an officer with The Gordon Highlanders and was awarded the MC. Since 1947 he has been a university teacher, and is now Head of the Department of Scottish Literature in the University of Glasgow. He has published seven collections of poems in English and Scots and is also the author of many plays, some of them science-fiction thrillers in English and others Scots historical comedies, including a satirical verse drama on the Trojan War, The Last Time I Saw Paris. *His many features for radio and television include the extended poem on Aberdeen,* Heart of Stone, *first televised in 1966 and since frequently anthologised. He is the author of a critical biography of the Scottish poet, William Soutar,* Still Life, *and has edited many anthologies of verse. He is currently co-editor, with Maurice Lindsay, of the quarterly* The Scottish Review. *He is married, with two sons.*

I was born poor, in a two-roomed but-and-ben cottage in the working-class suburb of Woodside on the northern boundary of Aberdeen, and I grew up in that northernmost of Scottish cities, unaware either of my poverty or of the richness of my inheritance. On my father's side I came of a long line of craftsmen and musicians. My great-grandfather, the soutar (cobbler) in the nearby village of Bucksburn, was also conductor of the community band; my grandfather, a ship's cook who had become a master-baker, played the organ; my

89

father, the first of the family to be born in town, was a power-loom tuner in the Grandholm textile-mill on the other side of the River Don from our house, and a soloist with the works choir. Everyone else, on both sides of the family tree, was sprung from the land, my father's mother the daughter of a grieve (foreman) from Huntly, in the far north-west of Aberdeenshire, my mother's parents both from farming folk in the lee of the Mormond Braes in the far north-east. My mother, too, had been a singer, meeting my father as members of the choir of the Free Kirk which both families attended. Like him, again, she belonged to the first generation of her family to be city-born.

But if Aberdeen was a city, the third-largest in Scotland, it was also a county town, a sea-port and a fishing centre, and from Woodside the countryside and the sea and the river were always in evidence. Indeed, there were still places where the countryside invaded the town, and my earliest memory is of feeding hens in a chicken-farm nearby our house. Some of the people were country-folk too – our next-door neighbour still wore the once-traditional tartan shawl. Even after we moved away from Woodside when I was three, and lived in the top flat of a granite tenement a mile nearer the centre of the town, the sea-links on the one hand and the open fields on the other were within easy walking distance, even for a child. All our early holidays, too, were spent on a farm near the tiny hamlet of Gartly, on the river Bogie of folk-song fame, and other early memories are all of country adventures, herding kye (cattle), hunting the half-wild bubblyjocks (turkeys) in the bushes round the steading, digging peat in the local moss and travelling back to the farm among the cart-load of peats, a tarpaulin over our heads as protection against a torrential thunder-storm.

Both my father and mother were what we called "knacky wi' their hands". He did all our shoe-repairs on his own last, and even in his seventies could build a garden-gate with as much celerity as skill, while she excelled in dress-making, sewing and knitting. Both, in their contrasting ways, were comely folk, he with glittering blue-black wavy hair, gleaming dark eyes, strong nose and firm jaw; she with fair hair, gentle blue eyes and generous mouth. My father also possessed a gift of physical co-ordination which made him a first-class athlete, a wizard outside-left at soccer, a demon left-arm bowler at cricket. If I grew up admiring (however unconsciously) formal excellence, that admiration was stimulated by their unemphatic but precise example.

All of us, and all our friends and neighbours and acquaintances, spoke the Scots of Aberdeen, and I was scarcely aware of any other language until I went to the local primary school, Kittybrewster, at the age of five. There the language of our alphabet-book was English, but the incongruity of using English in the classroom and Scots everywhere else scarcely impinged on me. Everything at school was new and different, and the novel language seemed all of a piece with the rest. I took early to reading children's magazines – first *Fairyland Tales*, published by D.C. Thomson, the Dundee firm that also produced *The People's Friend*, which every working-class housewife in Scotland, including my mother, read from cover to cover every week – and then their boys' papers, *The Rover* and *The Wizard*. The only books in our house were my mother's old school prizes, *What Katy Did, Rebecca of Sunnybrook Farm* and *Little Women*, but these I came to somewhat later, the first hard-cover publication ever to reach me being *The Rover Book for Boys*, a Christmas present when I was perhaps eight years old.

My father's baritone voice raised in song being a usual feature of our home-life, I had no inhibitions about lifting my own soprano whenever there was a singing-lesson in school, and the first distinction I was ever granted was to be singled out as a soloist at a school concert, again at the age of about eight. Only a little later, however, we encountered what was called 'composition', when the teacher would read aloud to the class a short animal-fable which we were then required to write down in our own words, and it soon became an almost-

weekly occurrence for my exercise in this art to be read aloud
to the rest of the class as an example of the result required.
This game of re-telling stories on paper was one which I found
not only effortless but also highly pleasurable, and I was soon
– if not simultaneously – practising it on the serial-stories in
The Rover, producing shortened versions of each week's
instalment of such fantasies as *Morgyn the Mighty* (a modern
Hercules) or *The Black Sapper* (a master-crook who invaded
bank-vaults in a sort of land-submarine). To me this kind of
précis work was sheer enjoyment, and it is only now that I
realise that it provided me – whatever its motivation – with an
education in seizing upon essential detail which I could have
gained in no other way.

When I was nine we moved again, this time to my paternal
grandfather's new bungalow in a district which was then on
the very edge of the town, on the one side fields that were still
being ploughed by horses, on the other a grass-grown cobbled
track that petered out into open parks which we crossed in
order to purchase vegetables (or to pilfer turnips) from the
first farm. The place was a paradise for boys, since the
wilderness – in the shape of disused quarryholes surrounded
by almost-impenetrable tangles of trees, brambles and bushes
– began less than half a mile away, with patches of wild
moorland and bog scarcely twice as distant. Explorers all, we
risked our necks (and our parents' stern prohibitions) to dare
those death-traps, and when we returned from our far-flung
expeditions it was to a triangle of waste-ground behind our
houses where a subterranean gang-hut roofed with 'borrowed'
corrugated iron and turf served as wigwam, igloo, castle or
cave.

Such fantasies also found their way increasingly on to
paper, for it was my great good luck, at the age of eleven, to
meet a schoolmistress, Miss Anderson – hallowed be her name
– who was in love with letters and possessed the gift of
recognising, and stimulating, such slight literary talents as
any of her pupils might possess. After school one day she

brought out from a cupboard a few copies of hand-written magazines which had been produced by various of her charges over the years, and noting my interest in these she allowed me to take them home to read that evening. In the space of a few hours of reading, the shape of my whole life was re-designed forever. Discovering that these magazines contained original stories written by their own youthful editors, I was stimulated to something of the same kind of "emulating vigour" with which Burns – in his far greater degree – had responded to his first encounter with the poems of Robert Fergusson. I too would attempt to follow where those giants of the past had blazed the trail. I too would become an editor and the author of my own fictions.

The first issue of *Schoolboys' Own* was ready on a Monday early in January 1932, some six weeks after my eleventh birthday, and it went on to appear at more or less weekly intervals for the next three years and a quarter, until April 1935, by which time I had developed from an amateur into a professional and was ready to move on from boys' fiction to attempt less juvenile themes. Since I knew little, and understood even less, about life's abundant actualities, I could not even begin to try to imitate or reproduce them on paper, and what I did imitate was literature, the only literature I knew at all well, wild-west tales, pirate yarns (the model here was *Treasure Island*, loaned by Miss Anderson), and ever-increasingly the school stories featured in such periodicals as *The Magnet*, *The Gem* and *The Nelson Lee Library*, where the English public-schoolboys of Greyfriars, St Jim's and St Frank's enjoyed weekly adventures which were equally free of parents and probability. For weeks on end, from one instalment to the next or from one "long complete story" to another, I would experience the vicarious excitements of a frontier scout in "Redskins to the Rescue", a buccaneer in "Under the Jolly Roger", a form-captain in "The Boys of Blackfriars" or "High Jinks at St James's", a schoolboy detective in "The Terror of St Tony's". Week after week, month after month, year after year, I lived their fantasy-lives along with my own, and week after week, month after month, year after year of my early teens, I perfected the technique of pastiche to such an extent that if Frank Richards, the creator of Billy Bunter and the boys of Greyfriars, or Edwy Searles Brookes, the chronicler of St Frank's detective-headmaster and his schoolboy assistants, had been simultaneously whisked away to that Beautiful Boarding-School in the Sky, then by the merest slight alteration of the names of schools and characters I could have taken over their respective series without their departures being even suspected.

Alongside this protracted apprenticeship to fiction, my experience of the drama was the briefest flash-in-the-pan, although here again Miss Anderson was the prime mover, arranging a class visit to the 'gods' of His Majesty's Theatre to see a dramatic version of *Treasure Island*. Entranced by its theme of boy-beats-buccaneers, I borrowed her copy of the book and set to work on my own dramatic version for school performance, but realising that the scenes aboard the good ship *Hispaniola* and the desert island would require stage sets far beyond juvenile resources, I confined myself to the chapters set in the 'Admiral Benbow' Inn, recruited a cast from my classmates, and produced the play before all the upper classes in the school on the day the winter term ended. The applause was gratifying, and equally so the appreciation of my modesty in refraining from casting myself in the part of the juvenile lead, Jim Hawkins (from which part I had withdrawn on realising that Dr Livesey, to whom I graciously diverted my thespian talents, had far more effective speeches). But seats at the theatre cost more than my parents could afford at a time when the Great Slump was drastically slashing wages, and the only other play I was able to see at this period – and then only on a free ticket – was *Peter Pan*, which I remember more for Jean Forbes-Robertson's darkly-elfin performance than for any persuasiveness in the action or dialogue. It was years before I entered a theatre again.

My performance on paper as a juvenile Frank Richards might have gone on much longer than it did if I had modelled myself on Peter Pan and refused to grow up, but this process occurred inevitably and inexorably, forever opening fresh horizons. The flooding of British bookstalls by cheap American pulp-fiction led me away from school-stories towards pseudo-scientific shockers, and through them I discovered the science-fiction of the early H.G. Wells and the exotic delights of futuristic disasters in far-off space. A short-story competition advertised by D.C. Thomson's boys' papers – which my parents interpreted as meaning 'stories *by* boys' rather than 'stories *for* boys' – resulted in my writing a yarn called "The Message from Mars" which combined my old interest in school-stories and my new interest in science-fiction, with an English public-schoolboy who won £100 in a crossword competition and invested it in a radio designed to measure rays from space. This I typed out on the second-hand typewriter which I had saved to buy at a shilling a week for a year, and although it failed to reach the prize-list it did result in an offer of a contract to write boys' fiction for Thomson's and an interview with the editor of their school-story paper, *The Hotspur*, William Blain (later the author of an historical novel about Dundee, *Witch's Blood*). This interview at the Thomson offices in Aberdeen, with Mr Blain suitably amazed at the extreme youth of his potential contributor, had two extremely important results for me, one immediate and the other far-reaching. While the editor accepted my story for *The Hotspur* (for a fee of £5), he did not renew the offer of a contract but rather advised my parents that instead of leaving school, as planned, at the age of fifteen, they should allow me to remain there for the full secondary course, when I should be seventeen or eighteen years old.

By this time I had left primary school and gained admission to Aberdeen's only free secondary school, the Central, entry for which was by examination only. This in itself was a new departure in our family, for my father had been sent off to work from his elementary school at the age of twelve, and my mother from hers at fourteen – and this despite the fact that her own father, moving into town from a Buchan farm, had eventually become janitor of this same Central Secondary School. But both my parents possessed quick intelligence, and my father's army experience during the so-called Great War, and his subsequent involvement in music, had awakened a wide and acute intellectual curiosity. They were determined I should receive the education which they had been denied, and despite the hardships that followed the Slump, with year after year when my father was in work for only two weeks out of every four, I remained at secondary school while half my contemporaries, at least as bright as myself, were turfed out at fifteen to struggle for employment at the end of their third secondary year.

When I went on into the fourth year, the depression in the textile industry had reached its nadir, and money was so tight in the family that I was wearing my father's old suits and flannel trousers, darned at the knees where they had become transparent from use. Yet I was revelling then in the consciousness of new beginnings. From the Fourth onwards, classes were co-educational, and almost immediately I became involved in a succession of adolescent pseudo-sexual encounters whose daft complexities might have bewildered Lothario himself. I also made a new friend, the painter Hamish Lawrie, who had only recently arrived in Aberdeen from Lanarkshire. A year older than myself, he was already alive to the intellectual and aesthetic challenges of the world beyond the classroom, and in the intervals between classes, or on our way home from school, we would sharpen our minds against one another in animated arguments such as I had never before experienced. And I discovered a new dimension to the world – history.

This was long before the revolution in educational theory which has resulted in the teaching of English in schools being geared to the immediately-relevant and/or contemporary, and

96

the prescribed novels in the Fourth were Sir Walter Scott's *Old Mortality* and *Guy Mannering*. Both I enjoyed – although aware even then of the constructional flaws in the latter – but *Old Mortality* made an impression on me, bringing to life an era of late seventeenth-century political and religious struggle, which has remained indelible. Perhaps, without knowing it, I was able to identify with the 'moderate' hero, Henry Morton, who found himself a victim of both Church and State, for I too was already in some kind of rebellion against both. Although, as the custom was, I had attended our kirk's Sunday School from the age of five, and my ability to read and remember and reproduce in my own words had resulted in umpteen prizes for Bible Knowledge, it had also led to an increasing reluctance to accept either Old or New Testament religion as anything other than a sequence of fine fables, and when I was twelve I had flatly refused to spend any more Sunday mornings on religious regurgitations. As far as the state was concerned, the Slump – and the sight of my father's near-despair at the forces which denied him a decent livelihood – had made me turn, as he did, "agin the government". Again without knowing it, I was one of a whole generation of "working-class intellectuals" whose political views were directed towards socialism by being compelled to watch their elders degraded by what seemed to be the utterly senseless 'laws' of capitalist economics.

With Henry Morton, compelled to renounce his allegiance to both covenanters and cavaliers, I was in complete imaginative sympathy. But over and above this was Scott's superb ability to make the past immediate and alive, and my enthusiastic response to that unrivalled gift, expressed in a class essay, led to our English teacher, Miss Forbes – another hallowed name – recommending me to read other historical novels, particularly Robert Graves's then recently-published *I, Claudius* and *Claudius the God*. However, such was the grip still retained on Scottish schools by the old gnarled fist of Calvinist puritanism that she felt compelled to insist that I never reveal the source of that recommendation to enter the brutal and licentious world of pre-Christian Rome, where power and promiscuity seemed to be inextricably entangled. Here, revealed to me in print for the first time, was a dimension of life which hitherto had been reserved for ignorant speculation with my male contemporaries and at least equally-ignorant investigation with such girls as seemed half-willing and half-reluctant to share my curiosity. I read on, marvelling, page after scandalous page, book after delicious book, crusading here, conquistadoring there, marching with Alexander from Macedon to the farthest edge of the known world, leaping in and out of bed and battle with each and every athletic hero.

In the Fifth year, while ostensibly studying for the Higher Leaving Certificate examination, I spent most evenings writing an historical novel of my own, *Troy Falls*. Somehow or other an ancient copy of Pope's translation of the *Iliad* had found its way into our house, and the fascination of the tale sent me to seek out and devour anything and everything I could discover on the subject of the Trojan War, from Euripides' classic tragedy *The Trojan Women* to John Erskine's modern satirical comedy *The Private Life of Helen of Troy*. My own variation on this perennial theme concerned a Cretan mercenary employed by the Trojans, shipwrecked on his way to the city and rescued by none other than the great Greek champion Achilles, then assisted to escape from the Greek camp by that warrior's slave-girl Briseis, and making his way across the war-ravaged plain to the besieged fortress, there to become involved with every Trojan character of reputation (or lack of same), including the notorious *femme fatale*, Cressida. With the introduction of this insatiably amorous female the author found himself in an insoluble quandary, for he had made his hero a moral paragon after the style of Rafael Sabatini's Captain Blood, while he had modelled Cressida on an opulently-bosomed girl classmate to whose charms he would have fallen an all-too-willing victim had she ever been inclined to exercise them in his direction. With the immovable object meeting the irresistible force, the action of the novel reached impasse, and *Troy Falls* ground to a halt around page 250, leaving its ethical idiot of a hero forever stranded in the lady's bedroom with one eye on her cleavage and the other on the door.

That same year, however, Trojan disaster was offset by Scottish success, when I was awarded first prize in the annual short-story competition organised by the school literary society, with "Blood in the Glen", a tale whose historical background was drawn from John Buchan's brief factual study, *The Massacre of Glencoe*. Again drawing on Scottish history, I wrote a Higher Leaving Certificate answer on Maurice Walsh's novel about the wars of Montrose, *And No Quarter*, where much of the action moves around an evocatively-described North-East landscape, including Aberdeen itself and many other places which I knew either from experience or by repute. The set question had required candidates to discuss some book on the Scottish scene, and by this time I was wise enough in the ways of examinations to angle it in the direction of my own interests. The result was an amazement, again altering my whole future, for it emerged that I had been placed first in English in all the city schools, and this pinnacle of achievement astonished my parents into the decision that – the worst of the Slump being over – I should not leave school at the end of the Fifth and try for work as a journalist but stay on for another year and then proceed to the even higher altitudes of Aberdeen University.

By the time this astonishing news broke, I had already been attracted into other altitudes. In reading for background material for *Troy Falls* I had become fascinated first by Greek mythology and then by myth in general, and soon I was eye-deep in "the matter of Britain", impelled onwards from Malory's *Morte d'Arthur* to the Arthurian essays in prose and verse of William Morris and his Pre-Raphaelite associates. Between seventeen and eighteen I awoke from the instinctive

99

existence of hobbledehoy youth into the conscious awareness of rawly-receptive adolescence, into aesthetic delight in the visible world around me and into a passion for the melody of words through which that joy might find expression. For the first time I began to feel compelled to write what I regarded as poems, as distinct from the occasional verse exercises – mainly atrociously flabby political sonnets in the Shakespearean form –which I had been scribbling at odd moments for some time past. My poems in the Pre-Raphaelite style, all adjectives and archaisms, were no less atrocious than the earlier sonnets, but at least they were written about scenes which I had witnessed with my own eyes, felt with my own senses. Of course they splurged uncontrollably in any and all directions, but so too did my undisciplined emotions, dazzled as they were by the sensuous riches of earth and sky and sea, flowers and trees and rivers, turrets and towers and terraces, whose impact exploded them into unimagined splendours. As if my eyes had been newly-washed in some magical elixir, I realised that I lived in a city of surpassing beauty, glittering in granite, arched by a dizzying width of ever-changing skies, the stone-grey sea walling the eastern horizon, the hills swelling darkly-green in all the other airts, the rivers trenching the bounds to north and south, glistening silver or brimming brown – and after dark, in the cutting clarity of the northern night, the steel-bright onset of the stars.

In prose, too, I was beginning to try to express what I had myself experienced, concentrating throughout my last year at school on a novel describing the developments of the previous twelvemonth. Here my model was a more modern aesthete than Morris, the author of a novel of English public-school life which, delineating the artistic experiments of a precociously-precious adolescent, struck so many responsive chords in my enraptured heart that the critical faculty was unable to sound a single note. The writer was Beverley Nichols, the book *Prelude*, whose southern smoothness of style was rather less suited to north-east Scottish brusquerie than floral decorations on a pair of ploughman's breeks. But this stylistic incongruity was not the only rock on which my novel *The School* was destined to perish. As with *Troy Falls*, sex would insist on rearing its adolescent rampancy, for in the period described in the book I had still been pursuing amorous adventures with any girl who showed willing. After the dawning of my aesthetic phase, however, those clumsy fumbling encounters in shop-doors, back-lanes and closes appeared lamentably lacking in artistic delicacy, and I turned my back on them, retreating into priggish disdain. The new puritan felt too much contempt for the old Adam to wish to draw an accurate picture of his pseudo-sexual activities, and this refusal to acknowledge fact ripped such a hole in the novel's heart that it fell dead beneath my feigning pen.

Not that all my artistic endeavours were entirely autobiographical and/or self-concerned. As 1938 darkened into '39, and the shadows of militarism deepened over Europe, Hamish Lawrie and I reacted to the increasingly desperate hour by adopting the pacifist position, and for the good of that cause we set about producing a propagandist collection of anti-war stories and sketches, *Down with the Pacifists!* Most of the sketches were provided by me, writing supposedly satirical dialogue in what I fondly imagined to be the style of Shaw – whose radical dramatic romances I was then devouring under the admiringly erroneous impression that their brilliance constituted an accurate reflection of reality. These were the first plays I had written for some six years, and they led me back to His Majesty's Theatre, where the Whatmore Players were starting a repertory season as remarkable for its range of plays as for the professionalism of the performances. But *Down with the Pacifists!* remained unfinished, overtaken by events when the invasion of Poland on 1st September 1939 ironically coincided, on the home front, with my receipt through the post of my membership badge for the pacifist organisation, the Peace Pledge Union.

Through another member of the P.P.U., that autumn,

Hamish and I featured among the founders of a study circle which she was planning to hold in her house, and the appearance at the first meeting of a neighbour of Hamish's, George Main, struck a rude blow against the flimsy façade of my super-aesthetic puritanism. Within a minute of entering the room, this boldly Byronic young man had us all in a roar on the question of free love and religion, with specific reference to the chairman of the P.P.U.'s local branch, a reverend gentleman whose family tree had been blessed by an almost-miraculous abundance of fruit. Since Freud, it seemed, sex had ceased to be smut and become science, and all of us nineteen-year-olds demonstrated a praiseworthy willingness to discuss it in the properly improper scientific spirit. After six months, the study circle disintegrated, its circumference having broken up into various heterosexual pairs; but it was all great and good clean fun while it lasted.

Apart from the psychology of sex, however, my aestheticism remained undaunted, and when in October I went up to the university in the medieval King's College in the Old Town I was enraptured by the opportunity of wearing the medieval uniform of the scarlet student gown. The poetry I continued to keep on spouting like a gusher was still redolent of nineteenth-century romanticism – although by this time I had got as far as the *fin de siècle* and was presenting myself in the role of "goat-hooved Pan", no less – and it took the impact of another new friendship to propel me into modern times. A bajan (first-year undergraduate) like myself, Tom Kennedy was the son of the socialist M.P. for Kirkcaldy Burghs and had gone to school in London, where he had already come in contact with the verse of the Auden/Spender school. Our discussions, and comparison of our 'individual' poetical attempts, eventually persuaded me that poetry had not gone into the coffin with Queen Victoria, and for the first time I started reading the work of elder contemporaries. Fortunately, the university library possessed the finest collection of modern poetry in the country, the gift of a graduate who reviewed for the

102

metropolitan press, and among all those heterogeneous volumes I was offered ample opportunity to try to distinguish between the good, the bad, the indifferent and the absolutely awful.

The summer of 1940 I spent on a vacation job in forestry at the tiny village of Durris on the bank of the River Dee some ten miles west of Aberdeen, where Hamish had found work after being thrown out of the house by a father furious at his pacifism (he had gained complete exemption at the conscientious objectors' tribunal). In the last year at school, and at university, I had virtually ceased to speak in Scots – except with my relations at home – but here among country folk I was back in a Scots environment, and this was probably the reason why I now started to study the work of Scotland's greatest rural poet, Robert Burns. Although my father sang Burns about the house at least as often as he sang the baritone solos in the *Messiah*, it had never occurred to me to equate song with literature – and at school, although some of Burns's poems appeared in various anthologies, they were ignored by teachers and examiners alike. Now, whenever we were driven to take shelter from the rain in barn or byre, I produced his *Complete Poems* from the saddlebag of my bike and resumed my exploration of this native exponent of a Scots tradition which was quite distinct from anything I had encountered in my formal education.

Those three months out in the open, watching summer slope towards autumn, were a new experience, and they moved me to write the first of my poems ever to achieve print, "At Summer's End", with its first line ("Summer declines like stock before fiasco") demonstrating that at least I had passed on from romantic pastiche to modern left-wing jargon. I was also passing on from pacifism. With France fallen, and the Battle of Britain raging in full fury throughout those golden summer days while I was putting the sickle to the weeds in long lines of young fir-trees, I reached the conclusion that while pacifism might just possibly work if it were practised by a whole nation, there was no likelihood either of it being adopted by embattled Britain or of its having the desired disarming effect on Hitler's Germany. After my twentieth birthday that November I registered for national service with the army.

Exempted until the university session closed at the end of June 1941, I set to work on the completion of an autobiography which I had begun at the age of nineteen but had given up at page 60 (when I had reached age ten). Probably the compulsion behind this was the feeling that since my Aberdonian youth would soon be over, I ought to put a record on paper before a different life in the world outside began to blur my aboriginal memories – and this time I reached age twenty, in four hundred pages. But the military authorities showed no impatience to avail themselves of my services, and after marking time over the summer vacation – during which I wrote the earliest of my poems still in print, "Song-Birds" – I found myself back at university in October, one of only two male students in the Junior Honours class of English Language and Literature. The other was Derick Thomson of Stornoway (now Professor of Celtic at Glasgow University, with a world reputation as a Gaelic poet and scholar), and he and I were often in animated argument over the relative merits of Scottish nationalism and international socialism. At the time, the international socialist – as I held myself to be – was quite convinced that he had emerged victorious from all the arguments, but the fact that it was then and only then that I bought Hugh MacDiarmid's anthology *The Golden Treasury of Scottish Poetry*, introducing me for the first time to both the medieval and the modern makars, shows the persuasiveness which Derick's friendly advocacy possessed.

My calling-up papers arrived on my twenty-first birthday, 28th November 1941. A few days later, "At Summer's End" appeared in the local literary and political monthly, *North-East Review*, and by the end of the week I was in the army in Yorkshire, with my apprenticeship beginning all over again.

ALEXANDER SCOTT

SELECTED BIBLIOGRAPHY

Prometheus '48 (1948); *The Latest in Elegies* (1949); *Selected Poems* (1950); *Untrue Thomas* (1952); *Mouth Music* (1954); *Shetland Yarn* (1954); *Still Life: William Soutar 1898–1943* (1958); *Cantrips* (1968); *Greek Fire* (1971); *The MacDiarmid Makars 1923-1972* (1972); *Double Agent* (1972); *Selected Poems 1943–1974* (1975).

7. Between Sea and Moor

by *Iain Crichton Smith*

Born in 1928 in the Island of Lewis, Iain Crichton Smith was educated at Nicolson Institute, Stornoway, and Aberdeen University where he took a degree in honours English. He taught English, mainly in Oban School, from 1952 to 1977 but is now a free-lance writer living in Oban. At the moment he is engaged on translations of Gaelic poems (from the sixteenth to twentieth centuries) into English.

Brought up on the Island of Lewis, I never left it till I was seventeen years old and went to Aberdeen University.

When I think of Lewis now, when I try to feel it again in my bones and flesh, what returns to me?

The moor and the sea.

I could never live away from the sea. Days when it drowsed in the sun, when among rank flowers we sat on a headland and watched the ships sailing by. Days when the rain streamed down the window-panes and the sea was grey and dull about the bare island out in the bay.

Days when the waves were playful about the rocks. Days when I used to draw drifters with crayons on a page of writing pad. Days when we used to search for crabs among the pools or sit on the pier swinging our legs watching the faint blue hills across the water.

Days in Stornoway when, a pupil at the Nicolson Institute, I would walk along the quay watching the drifters with their orange buoys and men seated, apparently sewing, among green netting. Salt in the nostrils. Herring in barrels. The grey shops crouched facing the sea and the masts.

Nights of astonishing radiance when the moonlight laid yellow roads across the water.

Many years afterwards I would think of my mother working as a fishergirl among these barrels, wearing her flesh-coloured gloves, an inconceivable girl in a world so different from mine, and I would feel guilty as if I had condemned her to that life.

The sea, monster and creator, has remained with me as a well of fertile symbolism. I think of the many dead – some whom I have known – drifting about in it, being refined there forever. One of the best footballers in the island was drowned there one terrible night. Another boy was blinded by an oar. The *Iolaire* sank there on New Year's morning, in 1919, bringing home from the war two hundred men to be drowned on their own doorsteps, a tragedy that breaks the mind. And yet on summer days how innocent it looks, how playful, how almost Mediterranean. How easily like a human being it is transformed from serenity to anger, from calm to sudden outbursts of rage. On an island the sea is always present. Always one hears the sound of it behind the painted day, a background, a resonance, the loved and feared one.

My house lay between the sea and the moor; the moor which was often red with heather, on which one would find larks' nests, where one would gather blaeberries: the moor scarred with peatbanks, spongy underfoot: blown across by the wind (for there is no land barer than Lewis). I am a child again, barefooted, jerseyed, bare-kneed, the daisies are growing, the daffodils are a blaze of yellow. The smoke of the village chimneys is rising into the sky. There is a vague desultory hammering, dogs are barking, there are cows munching clothes on the line.

Days when we played football all day, nights when we

played football by the light of the moon, returning home across the moor like sweaty ghosts, the moon a gold football in the sky.

How can one be that boy again? How can one walk home from the well with the two pails brimming with water, on paths that are probably now gone, between the cornfields, and through the long wet grass?

The moor and the grass and the sea. Throwing stones at telegraph poles, jumping rivers, watching roofs being tarred, hearing the lazy hammering of stones from the quarry.

The high sky of Lewis above the stones, the sea, the bleak landscape almost without distraction of colour.

And beyond it all on moonlit nights hearing the music of the accordion and the feet of the dancers from the end of the road, having thoughts of a warm eternity brooded over as by a hen with red feathers.

Later, but in Dumbarton, I would try to write about some of this in a complex of images which I called "Some Days Were Running Legs":

> Some days were running legs and joy
> and old men telling tomorrow would be
> a fine day surely, for sky was red
> at setting of sun between the hills.
>
> Some nights were parting at the gates
> with day's companions: and dew falling
> on heads clear of ambition except light
> returning and throwing stones at sticks.
>
> Some days were rain flooding forever the green
> pasture: and horses turning to the wind
> bare smooth backs. The toothed rocks rising
> sharp and grey out of the ancient sea.
>
> Some nights were shawling mirrors lest the lightning
> strike with the eel's speed out of the storm.

Black the roman rooks came from the left squawking
and the evening flowed back around their wings.

The phrase "and old men telling tomorrow would be a fine
day surely" refers to the one indisputably marvellous day in
the year. This was the day when we – that is, my two brothers
and I – were allowed a visit to Stornoway, seven miles and a
whole world away. On the night before, I would go and ask
the old men of the village, one by one, what sort of day the
following one was going to be, terrified in case it was going to
rain. And the following morning, how early I got up, how I
waited trembling at the side of the road for the first sight of the
bus, and then when Stornoway appeared, could Babylon have
been a more lustrous city?

Poor as we were, my mother long-widowed as she had been,
she at least tried to afford us that visit.

She herself had never been to a cinema in her life but she
allowed us to go. We ate ice-cream, we smelt the smell of
apples, we wandered among bookshops which appeared vast
to us, we ate chocolate, and if we were lucky we might arrive
home with small wooden carts drawn by rampant wooden
horses. And after coming out of the cinema we stalked about
the streets in a dazzle of heroism, guns strapped to our sides,
rolling on our tall boots along the grey pavements of
Stornoway.

And much later I would write about the cinema and about
Westerns, and about the Black Mask, Phantom and Spider
detective stories that I borrowed, and the smell of whose
yellow pages returns to me even now as I write. For just as
dearly as I loved Shelley and Keats – more dearly really – I
loved that other world of cowboys and detectives in their
lonely yet romantic settings.

I learned about John Dickson Carr, though not yet about
Ellery Queen, who seem to me to be the two towering geniuses
of the classical detective story. And about the same time I read
P.C. Wren and of course stories about the sea.

I read and read and read. I think I was really a very isolated child, isolated in school and perhaps in the village too: and isolated the more because I was often ill with bronchitis and sometimes with asthma. I was off school almost as often as I was there. In the long summer days I would lie in bed listening to the sounds that went on outside the house, in a dream of longing for some other world that wasn't this one, a world inhabited as much by English public schoolboys as by my own friends. My father had died of TB and my mother was terrified that I would also get the disease, so whenever I coughed I was immediately bundled into bed with hot water-bottles. Sometimes I felt so suffocated by this treatment that whenever I felt a cough coming on I would go into the next room lest she should hear me. I would spend days in the attic reading Chambers' Journals or sitting at the window looking out across the village.

In the village school I was slow at arithmetic but good at writing essays on the slates that we used then. I lived in a state of perpetual humiliation, shy and secretive, often ill, and when I look at the class photograph that was taken then, wearing my brown jersey which my mother had knitted for me, and a tie-pin at the throat, I see a child whose eyes are heavy and almost dim with fright, staring into a world which he finds threatening. Often I would waken at night thinking that I was haemorrhaging, for all around me the village was palpitant with the symptoms of TB of which the young and the middle-aged were dying.

When later I attended the Nicolson Institute in Stornoway a strange almost visionary thing happened to me. I was, as I have said, very poor at arithmetic and mathematics. Then one day I went into Woolworths and bought a puzzle book which I took home with me. I began to do the puzzles which were mostly, if I remember correctly, about differently coloured Easter eggs, and then in the morning I woke up and found that I could do mathematics, and that above all I had fallen in love with geometry. From then on I would do geometry

problems for pleasure and when the solution clicked so
elegantly it was as good as being able to write a poem.
Geometry appealed to some part of my nature which has to do
with a love of order and elegance, and also to a part which has
to do with a love of puzzle-solving. For this reason I only like
detective stories which contain interesting puzzles and also I
like challenging crossword puzzles. Even when I was in school
I was trying to do the *Listener* crossword puzzles though they
were pretty well beyond me. The idea of elegance would later
appear as the idea of grace, for instance in a sonnet like the
following:

> And lastly I speak of the grace that musicks us
> into our accurate element till we
> go gowned at length in exact propriety.
> I speak of the glowing light along the axis
>
> of the turning earth that bears the thunderous sea
> and all the chaos that might learn to wreck us
> if the chained stars were snapped and the huge free
> leonine planets would some night attack us.
>
> I speak of the central grace, that line which is
> the genesis of geometry and of all
> that tightly bars the pacing animal
>
> Around it build this house, this poem, this
> eternal guesthouse where late strangers call,
> this waiting room, this fresh hypothesis.

For many years the poem to me was to be an elegant
construction, not sweaty but pure, a musical artefact
composed of exact language.

One day when I was eleven years old and the weather was
blue and perfect the most publicly important and significant
event of my childhood happened. The Second World War
broke out. I remember that even at that age politics can't have
impinged on me suddenly and without warning for before the

war began I had written in Gaelic a poem about Neville Chamberlain setting out with his umbrella to shield us from the storm about to come. Even then I must have thought of him as a comic figure. But certainly at eleven years old I didn't realise what war would bring. Certainly it brought us gas masks which we had to try on and which with my usual clumsiness I found difficulty in handling. Certainly it would bring us saccharine and whalemeat. And we would wander about the village for metal scrap to help the war effort.

But it didn't occur to me then that it would send out long searching tentacles from vast unimaginable distances to pick off one by one a number of the older boys of the village who drowned in oceans which they had never seen before except on a dusty globe in the village schoolroom. Thus died Rob on a cruiser in the Atlantic. And many others. They would appear with their kitbags, home on leave for a few days, then later the telegram would come and they would never be seen again. My own brother was a lieutenant on a corvette and was later to be on a tank-landing craft at D-Day. We worried about him a great deal but we were also proud of him when he came home in his officer's uniform.

Nevertheless the war was in a way unreal. Nothing happened to us. No bombs fell on us. There were the RAF huts outside the village but hardly any other physical evidence apart from the black-out which protected us from the planes that never came. True, there was the Home Guard (or LDV) which my brother joined, once bringing home his rifle and taking it apart and assembling it in the kitchen in the light of the Tilley lamp, for we had no electricity. It was in fact difficult to get methylated spirits for the lamp, and that was one of the inconveniences of the war for us. Sweets practically disappeared, and everything was meagrely portioned out according to coupons. But nothing happened to us except that one after one the boys of the village disappeared to distant seas and some went down with their ships (for of course they almost without exception joined the Navy).

There was only one radio in the village (it was called a 'wireless' in those days, though it had wires) and it was, curiously enough, in a thatched house. Every night I would go and listen to it. It was perched up on a shelf with a white curtain around it and before the news began the curtain was pulled aside almost as if to reveal to us an idol speaking with a godlike voice. And certainly the voices that emerged from it sounded godlike, those of Bruce Belfrage, Joseph Macleod and John Snagge. They told us of Russian tanks chasing the Germans through the snow and of convoys being attacked by U-boats. Names like Timoshenko, Voroshilov, and Rommel became as familiar as the names of the villagers. The wireless, of course, had an accumulator and one day a woman from the village came into the house to hear the news but was told that the accumulator had gone down. "Obh obh obh," she said, "imagine that. And all the poor boys on her." For she thought that 'the accumulator' was the name of a ship, a cruiser perhaps or a battleship.

It was odd and disquieting to sit in that thatched house and listen to the news for one might hear of a ship on which one of the village boys was serving. One of the most ominous phrases that remain with me to this day is the one the announcer would use, "The next of kin have been informed". The war looked as if it would go on forever. And yet strangely enough it never occurred to me that we would lose it. It was like being in a theatre watching a play which had little to do with oneself, but which one knew in advance would have a happy ending.

The village became a world of old men and old women and girls. All the older boys had suddenly left. In the school itself we were mostly taught by women. In my fifth year I found myself on the magazine committee and was soundly lectured by the English teacher for having written a parody of *In Memoriam*s such as one might find in the local newspaper. Girls suddenly flowered into one's consciousness in their white blouses and gym shorts. Dido and Aeneas and their blazing love affair was projected as if onto a Lewis screen. The Latin

master, a ball of fire and energy, would stride into the room
and without pausing would say, "Begin translating at line
567" or whatever. The Gaelic poet William Ross died of his
love affair in a dusty room on a summer afternoon. And there
was a perpetual hunt for French irregular verbs. That was
what happened in the daytime. At night there was the thunder
of guns in the deserts of Libya while Tobruk was captured,
lost, recaptured.

Lewis of course was a bare island without theatre, ballet,
museums. There was a good library, however, and there I
would sit during the dinner hour reading magazines like the
Tatler bound in leather covers and seeing pictures of the
aristocracy bound together by a "common joke". One
afternoon I got so engrossed in a magazine that I forgot to
return to school till three o'clock and was saved from
punishment by a very understanding lady teacher. I think that
I liked the Nicolson very much: I became reasonably good at
passing examinations. I even tried the Aberdeen Bursary
Competition and won a minor bursary though I had great
difficulty with the Latin paper since all the 'u's had been
printed as 'v's and at first I wondered whether I had been
given a Hindustani paper to translate from.

I moved between the two worlds – the world of the school
and the world of the village – travelling home every night by
bus. At home I spoke Gaelic and in the school I spoke English.
But in those days I didn't find this an extraordinary situation.
I simply accepted it. I would never have dreamed of speaking
English to anyone in the village, and of course most of the
Stornoway people spoke only English. I wasn't writing much
Gaelic then, only English, and what I mostly wrote was poems.
There were no interesting Gaelic books for me to read, no
adventure stories, no poetry that spoke directly to me in my
own world. I used to read *Penguin New Writing* though I can't
now remember where I got copies of the magazine from, and
learned about Auden and other writers who excited me very
much.

I became, I think, slightly blasé in an objectionable and rather juvenile way. I began to think of the island as constricting. I couldn't but see that religion was dominant and often joyless, that ministers were considered as of the greatest importance, that certain people whom I despised were respected simply because they were church-goers and attended the Communions. It was as if I was searching for a wider world of ideas which I could only get through books, a freedom which I imagined as existing elsewhere. I felt myself as alienated from my own friends for I had the feeling that I was predestined to be a writer – a poet certainly – though I hadn't written anything that was of the slightest value. I even felt that Stornoway which had once been a pulsing city was becoming smaller and smaller and duller and duller. I thought of the black women gossiping at corners, in the biting wind, while at the same time clutching their black Bibles with black elastic round them.

I would return at night from the school and do my homework – I remember mainly geometry problems and Latin – by the light of the Tilley lamp on the oil-clothed table, and felt more and more a gap opening between me on the one side and my mother and brother on the other side. So I withdrew into myself and never discussed anything that had happened in the school as if it were a secret world which I treasured and didn't want tampered with at any cost. I didn't want to have anything to do with the cutting of peats, mainly because I was clumsy, but also because I felt that such tasks weren't important: what was important was the world of the mind. I was continually falling in love with girls who, I thought, were at least as beautiful as Helen, but I never told them my passion, I only dreamed about them.

The only contact I had with the boys of the village was through football, for I played outside-right for the village team. I was not particularly good but I valued the games partly for their own sake but also because by means of them I felt myself part of a team, of the village itself. Sometimes if I played well I thought there was nothing in the whole world like racing down the wing with the ball at my feet, the green dewy grass below me, and the possibility of scoring a goal ahead of me. I would listen to the radio and almost cry with frustration when in every game Scotland was hammered by a line composed of people like Matthews, Carter, Lawton and Finney. I couldn't understand how the English could keep their forward line intact throughout the whole war and thought that there must be a secret plot to keep these great and hated players available for the simple purpose of destroying Scotland.

I had no feeling for Scotland at all as a country except through football. I didn't feel myself as belonging to Scotland. I felt myself as belonging to Lewis. I had never been out of the island in my whole life, I had never even seen a train. Glasgow was as distant from me as the moon. I had hardly read any Scottish writers, not even Macdiarmid. Most of the writers I read were English ones. The island was in a way self-sufficient and there were even, strange to relate, many parts of the island I had never visited. For instance it wasn't till a year ago that I visited the district of Ness which is one of the most beautiful areas of Lewis. I travelled the beaten track between my village and Stornoway and it never occurred to me to go anywhere else, for of course hardly anybody had a car then, and we certainly didn't have one, we were too poor. My mother and the three of us existed on a widow's pension of about a pound a week and most of this was spent on food. I had no pocket-money for it simply wasn't available. My books I got from the library or from friends, one in particular who loaned me out detective stories which he could afford to buy.

In a strange sort of way too the island seemed to have no history. There were standing stones on the moor behind our house but I never found out why they were there or who had put them there. My curiosity about the past was minimal, and it never occurred to anyone to tell us anything about the history of the island. It seemed to have sprung out of the sea

117

fully formed, scoured by the wind, brilliant in spring with daffodils, without much animal life, and with few birds. It was a hard bleak island which did not reverberate when one touched it with one's mind.

Looking back now I think of its society as a very demanding one; classless, practical and in some ways claustrophobic. One was judged by what one could do, not by one's money (for very few people had much of that). The most important thing was to be practical and I wasn't that. I have seen men from the village building their own houses, which seems to me to be an astonishing achievement. They fished competently and did all sorts of jobs that I wished to do but couldn't; repairing fences, tarring roofs, cutting peats and so on.

I felt myself a dreamer in this practical world, naked and visible to it: and yet it was also a world that valued education not just because education led to a respectable job, but for its own sake too. Nevertheless, I sometimes have a nightmare in which I think that there are more teachers in Scotland than there are pupils and I yearn for the love of ideas for their own sake, for the free play of the mind.

As I look back on what I have written I wonder: what has Lewis given me? It gave me images of the sea and the bare mind. It gave me a respect for hard work and self-reliance and independence. It freed me from a trivial obsession with class and politics. It gave me a respect for clarity and I hope some depth of feeling. It taught me because of my poverty not to be interested greatly in riches and sometimes to feel that they are immoral. But I suppose that it also left me with defects, though perhaps these defects should be blamed more on myself than on my environment. It has made me, I think, unhealthily concerned with religion so that I find I do not wholly believe in poems of the moment, but rather in poems morally shaped. I find it difficult to be humorous and joyful in my work. There is a certain pessimism which may perhaps have to do with growing up among an ageing population so that I seem to know more about the old than I do about the

118

young. It gave me a respect for education which it took me a long time to free myself from, for Scottish education is simply one way of dipping into an endless sea, and that perhaps not the best one. It has given me, I think, a feeling for honesty and an unwholesome distrust of the Bohemian and the disorganised. The other kind of honesty that it has given me is more conventional, for there was no crime on the island. I don't think I ever heard of anyone stealing anything and of course there was no violence. Doors could be left open and when one returned to an empty house one found that nothing had been touched. However, I do not hear coming from the island the lovely cry of the transient but rather the proved monotony of the permanent. And in spite of all that I love the island.

I love it for its very bleakness, for its very absences. I think of it as a place beaten upon by winds, an orchestra of gales, which bend the fences like the strings of a musical instrument. If it has its noises they are not supernatural ones, they are in fact the noises of our own obdurate world. And sometimes, as I have said, the island will flower into the purest dazzle of colour, the more brilliant because the more transient. One of my more recent memories is standing on a road out on the moor and watching a man and woman cutting peats bent down into the rain and wind: and then suddenly a ray of light, fugitive and serene, falling across them so that for a moment they looked as if they had been framed in a picture without glamour or glory but rather attesting to the sudden moments of happiness or illumination that come to us out of the grind of existence.

When I was much younger I tried to put some of these ideas and feelings into a poem which I called "Poem of Lewis": I must say that this poem is a much more disillusioned one than I would perhaps write now, though it has a hard bleak truth, I hope, of its own:

Here they have no time for the fine graces
of poetry unless it freely grows
in deep compulsion like water in the well
woven into the texture of the soil
in a strong pattern. They have no rhymes
to tailor the material of thought
and snap the thread quickly on the tooth.
One would have thought that this black north
was used to lightning, crossing the sky like fish
swift in their element. One would have thought
the barren rock would give a value to
the bursting flower. The two extremes –
mourning and gaiety – meet like north and south
in the one breast milked by knuckled time
till dryness spreads across each ageing bone.
They have no place for the fine graces
of poetry. The great forgiving spirit of the word
fanning its rainbow wing like a shot bird
falls from the windy sky. The sea heaves
in visionless anger over the cramped graves
and the early daffodil purer than a soul
is gathered into the terrible mouth of the gale.

At the age of seventeen and sometime in October 1945 I left
Lewis for the first time in my life to go to Aberdeen University.
I waved to my mother and brother across the space of water
that separated the ship from the quay. I watched them driven
away in their hired taxi and as I did so I felt as if I were saying
some sort of permanent farewell. My mother suddenly looked
very small and distant in her black coat and my brother
withdrawn into a deep pathos of his own. I went down to my
berth and slept till morning and then when I went up on deck
in the dawn I saw a tremendous sea spreading all around me
and the sun as red as a banner in the sky. It was cold and yet I
felt exhilarated. A piper was playing on the deck. The ship
sailed on through that waste of waters till we reached Kyle

which seemed to consist of a flurry of seagulls above fishing-boats. I went to the train which was the first that I had ever seen. All day we travelled, first through stony land and then through fertile land over which the evening sun slanted, land very different from and much richer than that of Lewis with its poor huddled crops and its stone walls.

When I arrived at Aberdeen Railway Station the first thing I saw was a beggar sitting on the pavement wearing black glasses, with a cap for pennies at his side. I walked into the hurrying city with my case and took a taxi to my lodgings which were opposite the statue of Byron.

That night when I was lying in bed I thought I heard someone whistling a Gaelic tune past my window, but it was not a Gaelic tune at all. When I woke in the morning I felt no homesickness, only excitement. I felt free on the anonymous streets and because I was young I found my solitude exhilarating. The granite glittered from the large stone buildings, the trams and the buses passed by. I went to the university – King's College – which was anciently mellow and covered with ivy.

Lewis seemed a world away in both space and time. There were cinemas everywhere and a theatre. There were hundreds of shops, not the one shop which we had in the village. There was colour and noise. I didn't realise then that one couldn't leave one's childhood and youth behind one so easily, as if it were forgotten luggage.

And it came to me as a great surprise to hear some of the students who belonged to Aberdeen telling jokes against the city as if it were a small dull boring place which they wished to leave as soon as they could.

And yet years afterwards returning on holiday to Aberdeen from Glasgow I found it smaller than I had remembered. Nevertheless I also fell in love with Aberdeen as I had done with Lewis. The moor and the granite came together in a new synthesis. And here I really began to write poetry, a great deal of it about Lewis.

SELECTED BIBLIOGRAPHY

The Law and the Grace (1965); *Selected Poems* (1970); *Consider the Lilies* (1968); *The Last Summer* (1969); *The Black and the Red* (1973); *The Hermit and Other Stories* (1977).

8. A Man reared in Lewis

by Derick Thomson

Derick Thomson was born in 1921 in the Island of Lewis, Outer Hebrides, the younger son of James and Christina Thomson, and was educated at the Nicolson Institute and the Universities of Aberdeen, Cambridge and Bangor. He is now Professor of Celtic, University of Glasgow. The author of four collections of Gaelic poetry, and various academic works, he is married to Gaelic singer Carol Galbraith; they have five sons and one daughter.

The school and schoolhouse lay mid-way between the villages of Bayble and Garrabost, on the Eye Peninsula, in the Island of Lewis. It was a kind of no-man's-land, near the boundary of the Garrabost Common Grazings, where Bayble cattle might easily stray over the line, and where there might be small misunderstandings over peat-cutting rights. The nearest Bayble house was little more than quarter of a mile away, and the nearest Garrabost one much the same. But perhaps the schoolhouse was set apart in other ways also. One of my father's earlier successes there had been to help in putting an end to the battles with stones and slings between the Bayble and Garrabost boys, and to encourage football contests instead. Still, it was true, no matter how one defined it, that Bayble and Garrabost were very different places; that there was conflict as well as team-work; that people's different characteristics were deeply interesting; that there was a role for the referee.

The schoolhouse, in which I was brought up from the age of one (having spent the first year in the town of Stornoway) was a thoroughly bilingual environment. My father and mother habitually spoke in Gaelic to each other, but frequently enough spoke English to each other also, without any sense of strain. They had clearly decided to make English my first language, though Gaelic had been my elder brother's. I think this was a carefully worked-out policy, for we were in the midst of an almost totally Gaelic environment, and they reckoned that Gaelic would come easily. The only person I remember then who was not Gaelic-speaking was Nurse Cairns, who hailed from the Borders, and it was said she had a wonderful Gaelic of her own which she used with elderly monoglots. At any rate, English was my first language, and I remember learning to speak Gaelic, between the ages of four and six. Quite soon, and of necessity, Gaelic became the normal language between me and my schoolmates, and this happened also with my mother, while my father tended to use English with me. So both languages continued to be used freely in the household over all the years.

It was, as it turned out, a useful preparation for my later work. Perhaps some such possibilities were foreseen. My father was a shrewd, far-seeing man, deeply committed to his native language but committed also to the educational system he helped to run. He knew, in the 1920s, that of his four hundred or so pupils, probably half, possibly many more, would have to leave Lewis to find work. Many would go abroad, as his own brothers, sister, nephews, nieces had done and would do. He wanted to make the best of both worlds, for his fellow-islanders as well as for his immediate constituency. So he carried out his normal school-work, and in the evenings worked at other things: a school anthology of Gaelic poetry, which I remember him typing out about 1930; a collection of Lewis songs which he edited in collaboration with three friends; Gaelic sermons which he preached on Sundays and at weekday meetings when required; papers for the Lewis Association; his own Gaelic poetry. He was an elder in the Church of Scotland, Session Clerk, active in the E.I.S., in An Comunn Gaidhealach, cautiously involved in Liberal politics, but not a man of controversy (perhaps because he was fearful of a quick temper, and thought it was necessary to control it).

My mother was more reserved, supporting my father in his public roles by her presence and interest, and no doubt giving him the benefit of her reactions privately. But within herself she had an impressive sense of security and confidence. Her Christian faith was secure, and her Gaelic identity was secure. She did not have chips on her shoulder. She had inherited a fine command of Gaelic, and a good repertoire of Gaelic song, and loved both the language and the songs as well as the people they belonged to. She was greatly attracted to eighteenth-century Gaelic poetry also, especially that of William Ross and Duncan Bàn Macintyre. She loved company and laughter. Her training as an infant teacher had not interfered with any of these priorities, but she read both the Gaelic and the English Bibles assiduously.

From nine-thirty to four, in term-time, there was a hum of activity, chanting from the Infant Room, occasional loud teachers' voices escaping from the classroom windows, the triumphant roar of release at 'play-times'. I remember looking out at these crowd-scenes from behind the schoolhouse gate at the ages of three and four. Then after four o'clock, stillness, sometimes a huge empty school to play in, or later, to climb over its high roofs, always the hill and the moors. I became used to these extremes, and still need them both.

In my home context, however, stillness could be turned to advantage. One could read, or write, or think, or day-dream, and outside there was a world to get to know, flowers, shrubs, even a few trees which my father had planted, vegetables, vegetation, lichens, crops, animals, insects. The landscape became my intimate, each contour known and loved, many places stamped with their warm associations: the places where we waded in moorland pools filled with a spongy vegetation, in early July, and made piles of the stuff on the banks ('drying fish'); the Big Stones, a small neolithic circle where one could play rounders or practise running up a sloping stone and jumping off the top; the gravel docks in which we made roads and tunnels; the sea-cliffs for summer climbing; the wide moor where you could be a Sven Hedin, but all within the confines of a single day; the Polar wastes of snow where occasionally you saw a yellow patch, and knew that a sheep had become snowed up, but was still breathing happily. And the sea, always in earshot and in sight, seldom out of mind, the awesome Drowner, the maker of widows and orphans. We identified various women in the community in the 1920s as *Iolaire* widows, and the awful war-end disaster was often spoken of. But the sea itself, not that awful symbol, was a thing of infinite beauty and power and magic, that you could watch without tiring for long periods, and afterwards feel cleansed and exalted.

It was the common practice in the 1920s and 1930s for children to doff their footgear when summer came. My mother found it hard to agree to this before the end of April, but May, June, July, August and September were bootless months. For some families this was economic prudence, and there were some children who were without boots for most of the year, but for all children in summer it was a source of freedom and delight.

Lewis is a windy place. It was not difficult to feel that the whole island was in motion, being birled about in the general movement of the planet, and with a definite danger of being blown off, into the sea, into space. In winter gales it had a loud, eerie howl, which one grew to love. My mother used to put a coat over her head and a jacket over mine, and we would go out and stand at the end of the house for a while, in the dark, listening to the wind and enjoying it. It was a sensuous and emotional need, not like the doctrinaire theory of an old

DERICK THOMSON

Lewis bachelor of whom I heard, who made a practice of
going out first thing on a winter morning, in his nightshirt, in
the belief that if you got a good chill then you wouldn't feel so
cold for the rest of the day.

The sense-data acquired in these early years, and the
opportunities for observation, came to be of major importance
to me in my writing. Obviously this was not true in a scientific
sense – I discovered no leanings to botany or zoology for
example – but the particular sensibilities developed then often
served as a trigger mechanism for poetry. This may be
because I developed a definite reliance on imagery and symbol
in the structuring of my verse, but I am inclined to think that
this structure grew, partly at least, out of the data-bank of
sense images. It is of the nature of poetry, with its great
reliance on the subconscious, that the exact sequence of
development becomes difficult to disentangle.

It is out of that world, then, that many sense and Nature
references come, whether they come plain or purled. They are
plain in the first instance, an impression from outside of the
village of Bayble:

Bayble Bay below me, and the village on the skyline, the
eternal action of the ocean, its seeking and searching
between the pebble stones and in the rock crannies, and
under the sand of the cove: the everlasting movement of
the village, death and christening, praying and courting,
and a thousand hearts swelling and sinking, and here, the
plover runs and stops, and runs and stops.

Sense impressions may be placed, for contrast or for other
reasons, in a quite different setting, as in a poem set in
Glasgow:

I see the fields of barley, heavy-eared, and on my nostrils

127

strikes the rain-washed scent of autumn acres in my own country,
————————

Rough the stroking of the bearded ears on my hand
————————

Or in a much later poem:

I felt the rough side of you and the smooth
and was none the worse of it,
the two sides of the grass and two grips on the barley,
peat-fibre and moss,
and since the world we knew
follows us as far as we go
I need not wash away that mud
from between the boy's toes.
And now, in middle age,
I am going in to warm myself,
with my bare feet on a peat beside the hearth.

Often, of course, these early sense impressions flit in and out of a poem, like

———— the snipe passing by,
a swoop in the eternity of Lewis,

or

————grass and sweat, and the fragrance
of hair ——.

The "seaweed bubbling at high tide" becomes an aspect of the alcoholic's hallucination, and "iris swelling, yellow on a wet green bank" becomes an ironic gloss on a township's decay.

Many of the impressions are gathered in a seasonal structuring, in the poem "*Air Crìochan Hòil*", which has not been translated. And many appear in the sequence "The Far Road", which is both a celebration of Lewis and a farewell to it. Part of the farewell is quoted here:

[54] My back turned to my destination,
facing what lies behind me,
stretching and pulling,
on this thwart,
live-strength of sea below me,
muscles under the sea's skin,
my boat and my joy pulling on the same oar.

[55] Arnish light on my right,
Mùirneag cloaked,
a coverlet on the Barvas Hills,
a shroud on Hòl,
we grasp the bier-poles,
rocking and plunging on the surface of memory.

It was in Keose, in the Lochs district of Lewis, that I learnt
to handle a rowing-boat. My mother came from there, and we
often had holidays in my grandfather's house. It was built
literally on the sea-shore, and the tide lapped its rear walls.
He had had difficulty in getting a site on which to build when
he married my grandmother, who belonged to Keose. He and
my grandmother reared a family of thirteen there, and it was a
fascinating place to go to, for there was much coming and
going, of the family itself, and also of the village people, for my
grandfather, after starting as a joiner, had become an
undertaker, merchant, sub-postmaster and bus-owner, all on
a small and intimate scale. Before the road was built on the
south side of Loch Erisort, Keose was the 'port' for South
Lochs, and people used to row over for their supplies of meal
and flour and bran. The bustle began fairly early, at least
before my brother and I rose in the morning, and there was an
excitement in identifying the voices in the kitchen: Murchadh
Sheòrais Bhig in for his daily bottle of paraffin, with his high-
pitched laugh, the more ponderous accents of Murchadh Iain
Ailein, one-time deep-sea sailor, now something of a sea-

lawyer, *An Cat* (The Cat) who once conducted his own case in the Stornoway Sheriff Court, and referred graciously to the Procurator-Fiscal as "my learned friend", or perhaps his son *A' Phiseag* (The Kitten). There was salt dried meat hanging from the rafters in the kitchen, salt fish drying above and around the front door at the proper season, and great basins of milk settling, and turning thick in the warm atmosphere, though they were carefully covered with wooden lids and stowed in the lower part of the dresser. The cream would be skimmed off these basins with large scallop-shells, for butter-making, but also for *stapag*, a blessed mixture of cream and oatmeal, which acquired the most delicious and exotic tang when one scooped up a little of the thick milk from just under the cream layer. I remember once going to a house in Arnol, on the West Side of Lewis, along with my father and his brother Donald, who was a minister, and our first welcome was to have one of these large basins placed on the table between us, with three spoons, and an invitation to go ahead.

It was mainly from her mother that my own mother had got her songs, and my grandmother got them from various sources. Since her own tweed was waulked at home there was of course a functional aspect to the song repertoire. Her own mother was a Finlayson from Applecross, daughter of a MacBeth mother from there, so that there was a strong strain of mainland songs intermingled with the island ones. Women tend to be particularly strong tradition-bearers, especially of song.

There was a small inner bay behind my grandfather's house, largely land-locked because of the jutting tidal island known as Eilean Hàbhaigh, on which the Established Church was built. It was here that the Rev. Donald MacCallum, the famous Land Leaguer, preached to his small flock, and my grandfather acted as precentor, though he never committed himself sufficiently to join the Church. He and MacCallum were good friends. MacCallum had a large glebe, and ran it as a farm with the help of his brother Dùghall. Later this glebe was raided, and the village of Keose Glebe built on it. One of the raiders was my Uncle Willie, and my grandfather must have derived some real satisfaction from seeing his youngest son staking his claim to Keose land that had been denied himself so many years before. Nor would the irony have escaped him that he was now enjoying a few of the Land Leaguer's former acres.

Beyond Eilean Hàbhaigh there was the long sweep of Loch Erisort, where you could set nets (though for some obscure 'reason' this was not lawful), and some two miles down the loch was Eilean Chaluim Chille, St Columba's Isle, with its old churchyard. It had been the home in the seventeenth century of the Mackenzies of Achilty, at that time acting as Seaforth's factors in Lewis, and two of these have left poems, including a famous one about a boat *"An Làir Dhonn"*. We used to go there for summer picnics, and I remember taking my wife there in 1955, on a glorious warm summer day.

My mother's family had an effervescent quality, much conversation and a good lacing of wit in it. They resisted the ageing process to a remarkable degree. Among those still at home in Keose in the twenties and early thirties were Ann, later to be Stornoway's first lady provost (as Mrs Ann Urquhart), and Bella, who had a strong interest in literature. I remember arguments about religion, and my teenage view that the local variety didn't have any monopoly of excellence being regarded as heretical if not profane. I had already met both the spiritual and the pharisaical kinds of religion, and my views were forming quite definitely about both. Both were very strongly represented in Lewis, which is a place of extremes in any case, and my emotions are still apt to swing from admiration to loathing in this context, whatever my mind says. When I was sixteen and seventeen there was a strong religious revival in Lewis, and the spirit spoke in strange tongues and with alarming physical contortions at times. I think it was when I was in the Sixth Year at school that I pretended to have become a victim of this revival, and set about trying to convert a classmate who lived in mortal terror of conversion. It was a source of fun for those others who knew that I had not really seen the light. After that phase, our English teacher, James Barber, who also marked time as Religious Instructor, asked me to recite a psalm as a contribution to our studies, and having got his permission to do so in Gaelic (a language he had not learnt) I proceeded to recite a passage from Duncan Bàn's Praise of Ben Doran. Though I tried to disguise the rhythm I suspect he was not fooled, but in the difficulty of finding proof decided to let it go. James Barber was an inspiring teacher of English; he expected one to work and I responded by reading fairly widely, especially in poetry and the novel. His teaching of Byron and Browning was memorable. My Gaelic teacher, Alex Urquhart, communicated his own love of the language and its literature, and I regard myself as very fortunate in having had these mentors.

School in the form of the Nicolson Institute was an interesting experience. It was the only senior secondary school in the island, and one made the acquaintance of a large range of Lewis people. The school's methods were traditional: they believed in laying the foundations of knowledge and learning in a range of subjects, and they succeeded. I enjoyed school, and always feel sorry for those numerous unfortunate writers who had miserable schooldays. Of course we had no fags, except for smoking, and I never heard of homosexuality until later. There were girls in the establishment, and I lost my heart badly to one or two of them, and one in particular, but that was as far as it went, except that I had the indescribable pleasure of sitting next to her for a year.

The school had a small range of clubs. We played football and hockey and badminton, but not rugby or shinty. There was a Literary and Debating Society, with a Gaelic element in the syllabus but mainly English, a School Magazine, and a school opera production. I was involved in all of these activities, even playing a policeman in *The Pirates of Penzance*.

An ambition which I never realised, however, was to become a long-distance runner. After spending many hours in 'training', at home, I never felt able to take the final plunge. It took me many years to work that out of my system: I caught myself in my thirties thinking that this was an achievement that might still be to come. Fame on the football field eluded me also, though I once played for Aberdeen University 2nd Eleven against a team from a Mental Hospital, and eventually settled into the position of left-half for Bradford Technical College. Oddly enough, it was in that unlikely town I learnt to swim – it made a change from studying electrical theory in the RAF.

Unfortunately I did not have a long experience of my paternal grandparents. My grandfather had died long before I was born, and my grandmother died when I was five. I remember that it was always Gaelic she spoke to me, and that I could not follow all she said. My father inherited the family house, in Tong, and kept regularly in touch with the village. During the war, in particular, he took a hand in cultivating the croft, and he kept a small flock of sheep, so that I gained some experience with him of croft-work, scything, stacking, shearing sheep, fencing, and so on. There was a small nexus of Thomson families in Tong, as also in neighbouring villages, and another in Ness, all deriving from a common ancestor, a James Thomson (the same name as my father) from Speyside who had come to Lewis in 1737 as a teacher for the Society for the Propagation of Christian Knowledge. I have been told that his first station in Lewis was Keose, but he settled on the north-west side of the island. My grandmother, who was my grandfather's second wife, was a Campbell whose people originally came from Harris. There were twelve children in the two families. The uncle I knew best was Donald. He was my father's full brother, and they were close friends. He was at one time minister of the Highlanders' Memorial in Glasgow, and it was while staying in his manse that I learnt to ride a bicycle, in Lilybank Gardens where my university department now is.

But it is his Killin manse I best remember, the manse, incidentally, in which the New Testament was translated into Gaelic in the 1760s. We holidayed there, usually in alternate summers, climbing the Central Perthshire hills with our cousins Murray and Màiri, and sailing on Loch Tay. My uncle loved argument and discussion, in contrast to my father who was reserved or cautious in such matters. One of the things I remember also from these visits is the running saga of his battle with the Earl of Breadalbane over fishing rights on the Lochay and Loch Tay. He had no stomach for landlordly authority, and I think that the Earl, when he came to church, must have heard some sentiments from the pulpit that were not to his liking.

My Uncle Donald, though he was an active County Councillor in Perthshire, never made his part in politics very clear. There was a curious reticence among that generation over disclosing party allegiance. He would listen to my Nationalist arguments with great interest and good humour, and make an argument of it, whatever he believed in himself. I had become deeply interested in Scottish Nationalism at the 1935 General Election. We had a Nationalist candidate in the Western Isles, Sir Alexander MacEwen, and in our class 'election' then had returned a Nationalist candidate (that was in Class III). Donald Stewart, P.C., M.P., was in that class, and I am glad to say has since made the point on a wider stage. My interest in Scottish Nationalism grew from these beginnings, and I developed it considerably at Aberdeen University, and during the war years, reading the pamphlet literature and Scottish literature generally, and making the acquaintance in Aberdeen of Bruce Watson, Douglas Young and David Murison, all staunch Nationalists at that time, though Douglas Young was to try the Labour approach later. At Aberdeen in 1945 I launched and edited a short-lived Nationalist student periodical, called *Alba Mater*. We sold the first issue well, since many thought it was *Alma Mater*, the regular literary magazine.

Alba Mater was not, however, my magazine début. I had edited the *Bayble Herald*, admittedly for very local circulation, in the Bayble Schoolhouse, for several years from about the age of ten. This was a bilingual 'print', but the Gaelic part was not well spelled.

Local characters featured prominently, as was proper, in the *Bayble Herald*. The family, of course, had their eccentricities exposed by the Private Eye in their midst. My mother had a young girl helping her in the house at the time, and Barabal's father was the District Councillor; he featured largely also, as did Barabal. But none featured so largely as Cotrìona Mhór. She loomed large in the *Herald* for two basic reasons: (1) she was very large, and (2) large sketches of Cotrìona filled space when copy was short and inspiration failed. My brother James used to remark cynically on these journalistic expedients. For all that he was a man of action, given to playing 'soldiers' and 'kings' interminably, he had a deep interest in letters also, which eventually triumphed.

There was indeed some opportunity to study character, and 'characters', and Cotrìona Mhór was one of the most fascinating. Her great size anchored her fairly effectively to her own home. It was a red letter day when she occasionally appeared with her sister Murdag (Mucka to the family) to help with the school cleaning. Her help was mostly moral support, in the form of a running commentary. At home she had a great fund of talk, ranging from the anecdotal and gossip to philosophical reflections, and incorporating occasional folktales and personal reminiscences. Her Gaelic was rich and colourful. I heard her speak occasional words or sentences in English, and she could read both Gaelic and English. She had gone, briefly, to the old Gaelic School in Bayble, before the 1872 Act led to the building of the new school. She and her sister Murdag lived together, with a frightened cat; they were a devoted couple, and had entertaining domestic quarrels.

Another source of great characters was the visitors at the

communion seasons. There were two such seasons each year, at different times for different parishes, and this was an occasion for visiting friends in other parts of the island, and indeed in Harris also. The season lasted from Thursday morning to Monday night, and one might expect a succession of visitors, for dinner in the middle of the day, or for the night, or for the whole season. We would sometimes have three, four or five guests staying overnight, occasionally more, and perhaps as many as twenty to thirty for dinner on Sunday. That was especially so in the late twenties and in the early thirties. It was a privilege for a young boy to listen to the conversation, which ranged freely from sacred to secular. There was morning worship after breakfast, and evening worship late at night, with prayers, reading and singing of psalms (all in Gaelic of course), and in between discussion of sermons, both content and style, points of doctrine, fishing expeditions, current affairs, politics, and even an occasional game of football on a Friday or Saturday morning, before the visitors set off to church. This was one of the chief ways people kept up their friendships.

We had a full house of a different kind one night a week for some years during that lean decade from the mid-twenties to the mid-thirties. My father was a J.P., and had a weekly 'surgery' when men came to have their dole form signed. There might be as many as twenty men, in dark rope-patterned jerseys, in the kitchen, each waiting his turn to go through to the sitting-room to see my father. Though I was too young to know this in detail, my impression is that people were extraordinarily resigned, as though they regarded a minimal existence in terms of material things as their predestined lot.

We had many other visitors from further afield at odd times: inspectors of schools (Neil Gunn's brother John among them), occasional visiting lecturers – Arthur Geddes who wrote a book *The Isle of Lewis and Harris*, and who collaborated with my father in a play *The Spirit of the Tartan*, and the Finn,

Otto Andersson, who came to note down some songs from my mother. This was very welcome, for it added another dimension to experience.

The late twenties and early thirties saw a tremendous wave of interest in football in Lewis. This expressed itself not only in the relatively passive form of interest in newspaper reports but in the much more rewarding form of playing, and both village and district teams came into being. The local heroes, Sandaidh Sheòrdaidh, Suc, Alasdair Eàirdsidh, etc., had more fame than many national champions, Jimmy MacGrory perhaps excepted, and the matches were exhilarating in other ways also, in that the badinage on the touchline was full of interest. The basic terminology was borrowed from English but quickly assimilated into a Gaelic structure.

When war began in 1939 I was still enjoying that luxurious first long vacation after leaving school, and was looking forward to university. It was difficult at first to believe in the reality of war, and I do not remember having any patriotic sentiments at the time. For my father it was different, and though he had not often spoken about the First War, when he worked in the Ordnance Corps, and had been a short spell in the trenches, he was deeply interested in all the war news. Those who were in that war never got it out of their systems. I went to Aberdeen in October, and plunged into university work and life, taking Mathematics, Latin, Gaelic and English in my first year, and doing reasonably well in all of them. Peter Noble was Professor of Humanity, and he made Horace and Catullus live for me. Gaelic and English literature had already come to life for me, years earlier, but I enjoyed my university studies in these greatly, as also in Moral Philosophy which I took in my second year. We heard a little about Indian philosophers there, from W.S. Urquhart, but apart from that I became attracted to the strangeness of Tibet and India, and the long-drawn-out challenge of Everest. But the strongest influence on me at Aberdeen was that of Celtic John, or John MacDonald, Reader in Celtic, and we became good friends. When I finally went into the RAF in 1942, I spent my off-time reading Celtic, with Scottish literature and politics as a side-line. This left little time for radar theory, and when in 1956 I was asked by the interviewing committee at Aberdeen University about my rank in the services I had to tell them sadly that I had attained the rank of Leading Aircraftsman in the last weeks of the war. Magnanimously passing over this relative failure, they offered me the post of Reader, and I succeeded Celtic John.

My interest in writing verse must have been aroused quite early, certainly before reaching my teens, and throughout the greater part of my teens English was my favourite medium for writing. Then for a few years I used both English and Gaelic. I think the last poem I wrote in English (as distinct from English versions of Gaelic poems) was one written in Cambridge in 1948. Perhaps there was no necessity to compartment language and creativity in this way, though it soon became a habit. I suspect there may have been a palpable element of will in the original move to Gaelic as the preferred language, perhaps even an element of dogma, but that has long since become obscured, so that

> Now nothing but comes readier to the land
> Than this accustomed toil

(my reference is of course to the use of Gaelic rather than to the toil of creation). It might well be the case, however, that the decision on language brought others in its train. It is a matter of some surprise to me, for example, that I read very little Shakespeare now, though his poetry excited me greatly. I have often felt that to write poetry in English would have isolated me, imaginatively, from the community and tradition in which my imaginative life is rooted, but there is probably no way of proving or disproving this.

It is of the nature of poetry that all such experience, sensation, influences as I have been recalling, may be brought to bear at some time or another on what comes to be written,

138

sometimes in unexpected combinations. I found myself in Cranwell, in Lincolnshire, in the Spring and Summer of 1943, and there wrote a longish poem "*Faoisgneadh*", which is about Scottish Nationalist aspirations, but begins and ends with apostrophes to the Killin Hills, and has references to Douglas Young's imprisonment. The poem "Sheep" is much later, but picks up a much earlier impression:

> In the still morning the surface of the land was flat,
> the wind had died down, its rumbling and thrusting
> drowned under the whiteness, each snowflake at rest,
> set in its soft fabric like a white blanket.
> We had lost the sheep that were out on the moor
> when that storm unloaded its burden,
> and we spent the morning desperately seeking them.
>
> A storm came over my country,
> of fine, deadly, smothering snow:
> though it is white, do not believe in its whiteness,
> do not set your trust in a shroud;
> my heart would rejoice
> were I to see on that white plain a yellow spot,
> and understand that the breath of the Gael was coming to
> the surface.

Perhaps not surprisingly the data of sense impressions proliferate more in the middle collections I published, *Eadar Samhradh is Foghar* and *An Rathad Cian*, the former containing poems written mainly in the 1950s and early 1960s, and the latter dating from 1968–69 in the main. Political interests show up in all my collections, but acquire a harder edge in *Eadar Samhradh is Foghar*, and tend to dominate my most recent collection *Saorsa agus an Iolaire*. Religious imagery, and poems on themes connected with religion, become commoner in the last two collections. Both the Biblical vocabulary and the religious iconoclasm come out of that early world, just as certainly as does some sensuousness of impression and

139

language. And I hope I have retained a modicum of anti-establishment sentiment (though I have now become a proper target for it myself), and a touch of irreverence or mischief.

I have no doubt that the early years, perhaps up to twenty, are of fundamental importance to a writer, perhaps especially to a poet, and that this is a well that can be constantly revisited, not in a nostalgic sense but as a source of renewal.

SELECTED BIBLIOGRAPHY

An Dealbh Briste (1951); *Eadar Samhradh is Foghar* (1967); *An Rathad Cian* (1970. Translated as *The Far Road*, 1971); *Saorsa agus an Iolaire* (1977); *The New Verse in Scottish Gaelic: a structural analysis* (1974); *An Introduction to Gaelic Poetry* (1974).

9. Hard Times and High Times

by Sydney Tremayne

Sydney Tremayne, born in Ayr in 1912, was a newspaperman for forty-five years, chief sub-editor, then leader-writer, of the Daily Mirror *in London and later leader-writer of the* Daily Herald. *He now lives on the coast of Wester Ross.*

My father sat in a dark brown office on the ground floor of the Ayr district asylum beside a huge roll-top desk. Pinned at the side of the window a typewritten list said something about 600 male pauper patients.

Outside, in the pale spring sunshine, rooks were building in the tall trees. Their incessant cawing pleased me. Looking from the window while my father went on adding up figures I saw a party of women patients, two by two, taking their daily outing through the grounds. Their progress was slow, more tottering than walking, and their white faces had such a look of apathy and absence that I thought they resembled a procession of the dead.

All were dressed in black, from their identical bonnets to their heavy ankle-length skirts. I supposed that Arthur John, my father, had bought this uniform in bulk as cheaply as possible. As house steward of the institution he was responsible for supplies.

The men patients who were well enough to work on the

asylum farm and in the piggeries were also dressed alike. They wore shapeless dark grey suits, flannel shirts without ties and heavy black boots.

Many would cluster round me with pitchforks, eager to help the visiting schoolboy dig in a dung-heap for worms with which to go fishing. Bait was my usual quest, but in autumn I came in search of conkers from the big chestnut trees. I remember the energy of one ancient man, white-haired and white-bearded like a lean Santa Claus, who shinned up a tree with impressive agility and promised "I'll get ye more next year – if I'm spared till then".

I liked to visit the asylum, partly because of the novelty of making such excursions alone and partly because there was always someone there capable of mending whatever childish possessions I had broken. Usually when I called in to see my father it was because I wanted something.

My early childhood was a peculiarly isolated one with my younger sister Vera as my only playmate. My father and my mother, Catherine Sutherland, had parted for seven years shortly after their Edinburgh wedding in 1904, a fact which I learned only at the age of eighteen. My birth in 1912 was the result of their reunion. At first the reconciliation seemed happy, but not for long. We late-born children grew up guarded like the eggs of the osprey in a house which few visitors ever entered. If any stranger did come to the house, I was so shy that I ran away and hid under the dining-room table.

My father evidently considered that some toughening process was necessary when the time arrived for me to go to school. My parents were more apprehensive over this step in my life than I was. They worried that I was unaccustomed to other children, so a group was collected, goodness knows where, and brought to play in our garden. They were soon chasing each other, unconcerned with me. I was interested. I tiptoed around on the fringe, but nothing could induce me to join in.

142

That experiment was merely a failure but another effort to prepare me for the world had dire and lasting effects. My parents seated side by side, "Boys," my father informed me kindly but scornfully, "do not kiss."

I still wonder whom he thought I was going to kiss. Did he fear I might kiss the teacher, or the entire class, or was his warning simply a routine like squad drill – boys do this, boys don't do that, boys despise girls – a means of turning the unthinkingly natural into the naturally unthinking, suitable for society? If so, it was the wrong way to set about it.

For nearly ten years onward from that day, I blushed puce and suffered so much embarrassment that I could hardly breathe if anyone threatened to kiss me. Those who noticed this used to play tricks on me to watch the result. A mention of kissing was.sufficient. Love, as I grew older, was a word of such secret importance that I could not say it, rather as primitive tribes avoid naming their gods.

The cure of this eccentricity had to wait until I was fourteen. Vera was confined to the house with a gashed foot, injured by a broken bottle on the beach. Some of her school friends visited and we all played cards.

One of the girls, a blue-eyed minx of my own age with long, fair plaits, decided, no doubt encouraged by Vera, that it was time someone kissed the unkissable.

She rolled on to the floor, exposing navy blue schoolgirl knickers and white skin. Then she made her intention clear and I fled up two flights of stairs hotly pursued. At bay in a bedroom, I wondered why I was making a fool of myself. We did kiss and I liked it so much that I went in for the practice enthusiastically.

It was a wonderful summer. The daisies on the lawn were bigger, the grass greener and the sky more blue than I had ever noticed before. We were locked in each other's arms – Don Juan and Haidée – in cloudless and innocent pleasure. One day, as we kissed in the garage, I was caught unexpectedly by a too-Byronic physical impulse which greatly startled me, since at the age of fourteen I knew nothing about sex. This had not been included in my father's manly warnings. I held her all the more tightly, thinking it would be terrible if she became aware of my predicament.

When school resumed after the summer holiday, my Delilah said she had sprained her ankle, tied a handkerchief round it *outside* her stocking, and it became my chivalrous duty to carry her to and from school on the crossbar of my bicycle. I had an openly acknowledged girlfriend.

Vera and I were both sent to Ayr Academy which then possessed an infants' and a prep department, although it has these no longer.

The Academy in my time was ruled jointly by two rectors – headmasters in English translation, not clergymen. One, William Dick, was a handsome man who nevertheless seemed to have emerged from the taxidermist. He was all gloom and absence of mind and the story goes that he left his young son waiting on a railway platform in Glasgow while he boarded a train home, having forgotten the boy.

The other rector, Jamieson, was tall and spidery with an exceptionally long neck enclosed in a stiff collar that gave him the appearance of a giraffe popping out of a drainpipe. When he taught mathematics (my bugbear) he employed a roaring sufficient to drown the efforts of the teacher in the next classroom, and paralysed most of us with fright.

Jamieson, in spite of his menacing glare, was a human being and we should not have been too scared of him. He was intensely proud of the cadet physical training squad, victorious three times at the Royal Tournament in London, and it was because of this that I, for one, was allowed to spend days at a time in the gymnasium preparing for competitions, missing lessons which my teachers clearly thought more important if I was to pass examinations.

The establishment was the usual authoritarian Scottish school of the period. There I encountered the stodgier virtues which gave me a solid framework that I did not derive from home. Had it not been for school I would not have read the Bible and that would have been a literary disablement.

Whatever the Academy did for me – and it was much – it could not quite eradicate the awkward separateness which I displayed on first entering the infant class.

My mother made a bad mistake when I was enrolled, for in my hearing she advised the teacher not to worry too much if perhaps I did not speak at first. I accepted my cue and for the whole of the first term spoke not a word. I would not have thought of this idea without my mother's suggestion. While the other children wrestled in the playground I stood aloof, looking on. Nevertheless I was pleased when a small boy gave me a sturdy push in the back and said "You look like a policeman." I then played privately at being a policeman, which was a way of being included.

A teacher in the prep school, Miss M.A.B. Macphail, revealed to me at the age of eleven that I could write verse, and from then on I wrote 'poetry' and read everything that I could lay hands on, which was mainly the work of the Romantics.

While I was reading the nineteenth-century poets and novelists, hardly aware that the world had changed since Tennyson, it did not occur to me that life could be other than orderly. Indeed the rigid regularity of our home in Ayr's sedate Park Circus might well have seemed claustrophobic if my imagination had not been elsewhere. The poem "Stone Walls" reflects that atmosphere.

> A calm house for a child.
> Father and mother keep their separate rooms
> On separate landings. No one comes.
> The world outside goes wild ...

Every day at 4.30 pm we heard a crunching on the gravel path and Arthur John, our father, arrived home from the asylum wheeling his stately bicycle, a marvellous machine that looked as if it had been made by a blacksmith.

The chain was double the thickness of any other cycle chain

that I have seen. The bicycle (you couldn't call this a bike) was twenty-six years old and good for another twenty-six. The handlebars were high, so that the rider sat stiff-backed and vertical. When it rained A.J. held over his head an enormous umbrella while pedalling slowly with immense gravity of expression. This was a sight of some local celebrity which I have commemorated in a few lines entitled "A Sense of Balance". A.J. was pointed out as "the mad doctor" and this pleased him because he wasn't a doctor but would have liked to be one.

> Riding, erect and solemn, his twenty-six-year-old bicycle,
> Spats revolving in slow motion with the rat trap pedals,
> Our father, bearing his ample umbrella perpendicular,
> Ruled on the rainy road a wake of comparative dryness
> As he moved in his dignity through the slate roofed town.

Tea, inevitably with a boiled egg, was already on the table and we in our places when Papa (as we addressed him) appeared. After tea, at which there was little talking, he withdrew into his sitting-room and listened to the wireless, not yet known as 'radio' except in America. Headphones sealed him off from communication.

At seven o'clock exactly he left for his club and the household relaxed. Once he forgot something, returned unexpectedly, and looked bewildered to find us bawling "Duncan Gray cam' here to woo" in hysterical relief at his departure. At eleven o'clock his key would be heard in the front door and this was the signal for us to scamper upstairs and into bed so that we did not see him again until next morning.

Our main difficulty with A.J. as a father, even an indulgent father, was that he would not allow his children to grow up. I was given tuppence a week for pocket-money as a small child, and it was still tuppence, handed over with ceremony on Saturday, when I reached the rugby-playing stage and made trips with the team to Glasgow. I declined to accept this bounty any more and that was that. I did not ask for a larger sum. I said just that I did not want it, thank you.

The world opened out for me at the age of thirteen when I was presented with a bicycle and this gave me the freedom of the countryside. The state of mind into which I was precipitated might be described as one of quiet, alert and secret ecstasy. Or, why not, pure joy. The experience has irradiated my whole life.

Wherever there was a river, I wanted to go to its source. I investigated the Doon, the Ayr and its tributary the Coyle, but in particular I haunted an insignificant burn which joins the Doon near Minishant. I followed this to its beginning in shallow, reedy Red Moss Loch above Culzean Bay where ducks rose with a whirr of wings and cock grouse shouted their "go back" alarm, which I heard then for the first time.

I saw my first heron and ran after it to get a better look. I discovered in a hollow tree two white, hissing owlets surrounded by the corpses of rats and young rabbits. I made friends with a village boy named Henry and roamed with him barefoot in the hills through warm bog-water up to our knees. I was in tune with everything I saw. Rain sweeping, silver, across a shadowy hillside, heavy snow scudding before the wind almost blotting out the landscape, a great salmon leaping with a swirl and splash in the Doon – all these were excitements of the spirit.

I could not foresee how brief that spell of heightened sensibility was to be. In fact it lasted barely three years. In 1927 my serene dreaming in Scotland came to an end, my schooldays were abruptly broken off and with them my expectation of going on to university with my friends.

In that year my father threw up his job at the asylum, or was thrown out of it, after some disagreement never explained to me. He next bought an hotel in Harrogate, under the erroneous impression that having run a mental institution he was just the man to cater for the public.

The house in Park Circus was sold privately and there was

to be an auction of the contents after we had gone. Since the hotel was already full of furniture there was no room for possessions of ours.

Before the auction my sister and I silently surveyed our personal relics laid out neatly on the dining-room floor. Here was her array of dolls and there were all my books, Christmas presents which admittedly I no longer wanted, titles like *The Blue Book of British Naval Battles* and *Famous Regiments of the British Army*. Such had been my father's gifts to his son. I had no further use for such literature, but my name was inscribed in each volume. I tore out the inscriptions.

It was still more startling to see my cricket-bat, rugby-ball and the cherished boxing-gloves which had done much to give me a sense of identity. I felt as though I myself had been consigned to the past, all my former life spread out for disposal.

The piano on which I learned to play was included in the sale. It was a concert grand, presumably once belonging to my father's mother. Years later I realised it to have been a similar instrument to that played by Chopin.

I laughed a strained and would-be cynical laugh at my mixed emotions, reminding myself that I was almost sixteen years old. "It's the end of childhood all right," I muttered sententiously to Vera, who did not answer. I rescued only *Poems of Today* which I still have with a stamp inside it saying "Cambridge Hotel". My bicycle and golf clubs were the only other personal belongings that went with me.

Departure had inevitably to end in farce. My father was already in Harrogate, installed in his hotel. My mother and I were to follow, dropping our key behind us through the letter-box.

A horse-drawn cab arrived to take us to the train, but we had an encumbrance, a large parrot cage. The cabby gave it a horrified stare and declared firmly "I'm no taking *that*. I'm no having *that* beside me." It would have affronted his dignity.

Then he changed his mind. "I'll take yon thing or yous. I'm

no taking both." We were already locked out of the house. The circumstances were more like an expulsion than a removal.

The cage was placed inside the cab and the man drove off with it. We ourselves had to run all the way to the station with the parrot in a cake box.

I had determined beforehand not to look back at the house. In the event, bolting with the parrot under my arm, there was no time to.

In this way I was removed from Scotland and it took me forty-eight years to get back again permanently, to the remote house in Wester Ross where my wife and I now live.

In Harrogate I was dejected and homesick. A year went by in which I spoke not one syllable to anyone of my own age. I was reduced by loneliness to grinning in the street at unknown youngsters who obviously thought I must be insane. Eventually my father succeeded in placing me as the most junior of would-be reporters on the *Yorkshire Evening News* in Leeds, and a new life began. Everyone was kind to my inexperience and I learned quickly, but when I had been on the paper eighteen months I knew only too clearly that Arthur John's ridiculous hotel venture was in the last paroxysm of collapse.

My nerves were at snapping point. My pay was thirty shillings a week and if I had to provide a refuge for my mother and sister I calculated that I could not do it, even in those days, on less than £2. The dilemma was solved unexpectedly at almost the last moment. The proprietor of a weekly paper recently launched in the town, a man whom I had not met, called at the hotel and invited me to join his staff at the magic figure of £2 which I needed. For eleven shillings weekly I rented a room overlooking the famous Valley Gardens and waited for what would happen.

My mother was absent at this time, ostensibly on a holiday visit to her sister. In fact she had been driven from the hotel by her husband's hostility. I did not realise that he had formed an association with a chambermaid, a sullen, smartly-dressed girl nearly six feet tall, but this soon became evident.

In the last few days before the hotel closed my mother returned. Vera and I met her at the station and we were all talking in my mother's bedroom when Arthur John burst in, dancing with ferocity. He rushed straight at my mother and grabbed her by the neck. I happened to hold a large tin of floor polish in my hand and with this I hit him on the jaw with all my force. I was sickened by quarrels and would normally go to great lengths to avoid them, but this time I really meant to knock him flat. The impact dented the polish tin until one side almost met the other, yet he remained on his feet. He was dazed, though, and I was able to push him out through the door, which was swiftly and prudently locked behind us.

In the corridor the tall chambermaid bore down upon me brandishing two heavy glass vases, each two feet long. Plainly she intended to break these over my head.

This Medusa, with protruding eyeballs and venomous snarl, was like something out of a Hollywood gang fight. I can see the spectacle still with no effort of imagination. Luckily I managed to disarm her without becoming a hospital case. My father and she then withdrew and I was relieved to see them go.

That episode of violence might have been my final parting from my father – it was the last that my mother saw of him – but there was a sequel a few days later. As my mother and I were trying to arrange a few items of furniture in the room I had opportunely rented, Vera, who had gone out, returned with a message. Arthur John wanted me to go and see him to say goodbye.

I replied that I hoped never to set eyes on him again and had no intention of approaching within a mile. All I wanted was that he should clear out of our lives and never come back.

It was my mother who persuaded me that I must meet him, saying, "He is your father. It would be wrong to separate on bad terms."

I made my way to the detested hotel. The street door was

locked. It was unusual to have to stand outside and ring the bell. Arthur John came down to let me in. The dangerous chambermaid and the rest of the staff had departed and he would not be telephoning the Labour Exchange for more.

I followed him up the now uncarpeted stair and along the bare, echoing boards of the hall into what had been the public lounge. Our voices resounding through the empty building gave me an impulse to whisper, as though we risked being overheard.

In the lounge he had a bed and a chair, nothing else. The curtains had been stripped from the windows, the pictures from the walls. His mother's pictures. It was a pitiable sight, but he was a little too conscious of the pathos. He had already made a strong impression on Vera's emotions. It seemed almost that he had cast himself in the rôle of Lear and was watching himself perform. I was gruff and monosyllabic. It would have been undignified to weep.

I recall little of what was said. He did not explain where he was going and I did not ask; it was for him to volunteer confidences if he wished. He did, however, give me some information I had not known, and made a point of stressing it. This was the occasion when I learned from him that my mother had left him soon after their wedding and stayed away for seven years. I do not know whether he was trying to justify himself in some way or possibly hoping to damage my regard for my mother, who had now sent me to him. It is impossible to say what was going on in his mind at that moment, but it was an acknowledgement that everything had been wrong between them from the start.

My visit to the hotel that last evening was brief. The encounter was depressing and as dusk fell I realised that the lighting had been cut off. Vera went back a second time that night to collect a pair of gloves she had perhaps deliberately left behind, and the picture stayed with her of moonlight through the curtainless windows falling across the empty rooms.

My father and I shook hands. I descended the stair and as the street door banged and reverberated behind me for the last time I had a feeling of relief.

The remnant of our family now plunged from the false sense of security nurtured by Park Circus to the life of the shifting, the shifty and the near-penniless in that time of the big slump. The house beside the Valley Gardens was full of people living in single rooms and carefully ignoring their neighbours. I felt that I was living in a Russian novel.

With the resilience of eighteen years I was nevertheless happy in my sense of independence. I believed that everything was coming right.

By contrast, my mother hid from sight. She went nowhere without Vera and never appeared on the landing unless leaving the house. It was at this time that she developed the idea of pretending to be a foreigner who could not speak English. She kept this up later and it proved an effective way of defeating doorstep salesmen and other unwanted callers.

In spite of my optimism, our affairs did not come right. The new paper died six months after I joined it. With £2 in my hand, I was out of work.

I went home and wrote to every newspaper I had ever heard of, some sixty of them. As the days passed, I reconnoitred the Labour Exchange. There was an immense queue stretching round the corner and far down the street. False pride would not let me join this drab procession. I feared that I would be submerged for ever if I enrolled in that army of defeat. As a juvenile, I supposed that I might have received seven shillings and sixpence a week, which would not have paid the rent. My eyes filled with stinging tears of humiliation and I bolted. (This incident, recollected in tranquillity, made the poem "Slump".) I returned home and flung myself on the bed, saying nothing of where I had been.

Each morning I went down to the hall to collect handfuls of letters, replies to my applications for work. All refusals. The volume of my correspondence attracted the attention of somebody else. One sunlit day as I sat by the open window a torn scrap of blue paper fluttered on to the sill. Unmistakably the handwriting was that of my aunt. It proved that someone in the house was stealing letters. Worried in case I might lose one that offered work, I called the police. Consternation was caused when a detective turned up to make enquiries, but there were no results.

Days later a letter did come, from the editor of the *Goole Times* – God bless Goole – appointing an interview. It was a roundabout place to reach from Harrogate and meant catching a train very early. Nobody heard the alarm-clock and when I awoke it was nearly time for the train to depart. Flinging on my clothes almost whimpering in panic, grabbing a collar and tie and thrusting them into my pocket, and without time even to brush my hair, I must have run the first four-minute mile to the station, uphill at that. I tumbled into a compartment just before the train pulled out.

At Goole I was hungry, having missed my breakfast of porridge. I could not afford lunch but bought half a dozen bananas and wolfed these in the park while awaiting the time of the interview. My sprint proved worthwhile, for I was appointed the Selby district correspondent of the *Goole Times* group of weeklies at £3 a week.

Troubles were not over, because there was a month to wait before the job was vacant and our cupboard was almost bare. We survived that month on lentil soup and porridge.

I had acquired a girlfriend in Harrogate; vivid, dark and fiery, a child barely out of school, which is to say two years younger than myself. She was my sole companion. We had for two years considered ourselves pledged to marry and this we did on the day of my departure for Selby. Two rash romantics were formally united at Knaresborough register office, a bare and cheerless room attached to the workhouse and decorated, if that is the word, with photographs of bearded worthies of the old board of guardians. My mother and sister acted as witnesses. Although this juvenile marriage came to grief many

153

adventures later, my seventeen-year-old bride of long ago earned my admiration then and retains it.

At this point of my launching into the wide world I shall draw an arbitrary line and declare that marriage marked the end of adolescence, although I doubt that in fact it did so. It did signal the start of a whirlwind, restless period that carried me before the war in my twenties into the chief sub-editor's chair of the wildest and noisiest newspaper in Fleet Street, and after the war, as that journal's leader-writer, into resounding collision with one Winston Churchill. But such events are outside the scope of these reminiscences of youth.

I had no chance to be a precocious poet. My first volume, born in the joy of my second marriage, was not published until I was released from the fire service at the end of the war. It resulted from my sending only six poems to a well-known publisher which brought a telegram in reply – unhoped-for encouragement. This book, and that which immediately followed it, were written in the quiet hours before dawn when I reached home at two o'clock in the morning from my labours in the newspaper office. Both books ran to sixty-four pages and the second was written in fifteen months, blown along recklessly fast in a burst of creative excitement.

It will be evident from the history I have now disclosed, if it was not already obvious, that very many of my poems took their shape from life, although the impulse was not directly or merely autobiographical. I wrote, not to explain something to anyone else, but to investigate what truth might be found in the inner life of poetry. I put this badly, but no one should ask *why* a poet writes because no glib answer is possible.

Certainly I had no desire to be a public oracle. Having to deal day by day in prose with what John Betjeman calls "burning issues", I was freed from the temptation of opinionated versifying: poetry of any interest to me is more subtle and does not have designs upon an audience. Poems are discoveries. If I knew beforehand where a poem was going to lead I would never start writing.

I need say no more about the poems which are openly autobiographical, except perhaps to confirm that "Details from a Death Certificate" is a meditation upon the harsh fate of my father, whose ending was unknown to me for nine years. Unknown also to my mother, whose death caused me to search for information about him at Somerset House. The poem "Endings" arose from recollection of the Harrogate period.

I may be blamed by some for rattling private skeletons in public, but these are very old skeletons. If poetry is published it is legitimate, and anyway inevitable, that readers should be curious to know more about it, and in the present case there is nobody alive whom the story can hurt.

> What is done is done, is done
> Shouts the starling in the sun.
> Belsen's buried in the brain:
> Roots that thirst like weasels rip
> Earth and what earth covers up.
> Every crime and more to come
> Is the promise of each time
> Yet the world outlives the lot.
> Generations are on heat:
> In shining ignorance like flame
> The newest creatures, without blame,
> Rise in vigour of their blood
> To stalk each other through the wood.
> Constantly the world disowns
> Canting sermons upon stones
> And consumes its rotten bones.
> Mind draws nothing, the sun must,
> From the past's explosive dust.

SELECTED BIBLIOGRAPHY

Time and the Wind (1948); *The Hardest Freedom* (1951); *The Rock and the Bird* (1955); *The Swans of Berwick* (1962); *The Turning Sky* (1969); *Selected and New Poems* (1973).

10. My Many Splendoured Pavilion

by Fred Urquhart

Fred Urquhart earned his living for many years as a reader and editor for a number of London publishers. His stories have appeared in most of the well-known British and American literary periodicals and in many anthologies. The Ploughing Match *won the Tom Gallon Award in 1951. He received bursaries from the Arts Council in 1966 and the Scottish Arts Council in 1975. He edited a cartoon biography of Winston Churchill, and co-edited* No Scottish Twilight *with Maurice Lindsay and* Modern Scottish Stories *with Giles Gordon. He has lived in Sussex for over twenty years but has never lost his Scottish accent.*

Love, the singer tells us, is a many-splendoured thing. This splendid phrase aptly describes my early days which were multi-coloured by the legend of the Urquhart Millions. Although my family was poor in worldly goods, we were not poor in spirit, for the legendary millions always spun in the sky before us: a coloured ball like one of these gaily-stranded paperweights, whirling and whirling, luring us on with its rich promises, making me feel that the future – and the very near future at that! – would be so grand that the present was negligible. I knew that, soon, I would be pavilioned in splendour and girded with praise. I had never heard of Sir Robert Grant and did not realise that it was God and not me he was writing about in his hymn.

After *Time Will Knit* was published in 1938, a bookseller friend told me that one of yon awful multitude of Edinburgh's prim and proper ladies, with nebs reddened by repression and the eternal east wind, had come into his shop and announced: "This book should be flung back in the gutter beside its author. It's where he belongs."

The dear soul was wrong. I was brought up among the gentry. I moved with ease between the seats of the mighty and the stools of the lowly. When I was six I sat on the lap of the Marchioness of Breadalbane at a children's Christmas party at Taymouth Castle and told her I was going to be a great artist. The following summer I sat on the doorstep of my maternal grandmother's cottage overlooking Granton Harbour and read passages from a serial by Annie S. Swan in the *People's Friend* to her and several other admiring auld wifies who said I was a clever wee laddie and would go far.

I never saw my grandfather Urquhart. He died before I was born. His name was William, and he was one of the sons of an innkeeper in the Black Isle of Ross and Cromarty. I know nothing of my great-grandfather, but I think he must have been an auld devil, well endowed with the Urquhart temper, which goes up like a flash but subsides as quickly. One of his sons, John, emigrated after a row with his father and landed in either Canada or Australia – the family never seemed able to make up its mind about the exact place – and joined the gold rush. To prove to my great-grandfather that he hadn't gone to the bad, as predicted, he wrote home once to say he'd struck it rich. He is believed to have made a fortune, hence the legend of the Urquhart Millions. From time to time, all through my childhood, there were pieces in Scottish newspapers about these millions and the search for missing heirs, and always our hearts leapt with joy. Now that age and knowledge of the newspaper world has made me cynical, I believe these reports were fomented by people like my Auntie Meg, an incurable romantic. But being a romantic myself, I sometimes still have a small half-hearted hope that it might all come true and that reporters don't always make up things from auld wives' tales and that vast sums of money, swollen beyond avarice with the years, are waiting in the vaults of New York or Melbourne for the Urquharts to claim them. Though I always add a rider to these thoughts that my own share might not amount to much as my father was the youngest son of a younger son and I have countless cousins.

William Urquhart followed brother John's example. He ran away, aged fourteen, and joined the army. He became a boy trumpeter and, still in his teens, played a solo before Queen Victoria. Whether the old lady was impressed or not, I don't know. I have a miniature that shows him as a thin-faced, clean-shaven dark young man in uniform, wearing a pillbox hat cocked to the side, the kind they used to wear in the Boys' Brigade. William's father tried to buy him out, then he wanted to buy him a commission, but Auld Willie, as his family always referred to him (and not often with kindness) refused to rise in rank or leave the army, which next to music was his great love. He spent the last years of his life as Bandmaster of the regiment known as the Duke's Canaries at Glencorse Barracks in Midlothian.

My other grandfather, Robert Harrower, had a wooden leg. His leg was sawn off by primitive surgery without an anaesthetic when Bob had an accident as a young ship's carpenter. The stump caused him great pain in his last years, though he lived to be ninety; he was always getting cramp in it, and I can remember watching it jump up and down while he strove to hold it steady, his face screwed up in agony. When I was a little boy he was ending his working life as foreman of the sawmill at Granton. He was then about the age I am now. Bob was a very good-looking old man with well-brushed white hair and beard. I used to watch with grave attention when he massaged his scalp every morning with a brown liquid called Thatcho that was intended to retain his hair. Alas, I have never used Thatcho!

My grandmother, Williamina Morrison, was one of the

three daughters of a sea captain from Burntisland, who was for a long time skipper of the *William Muir*, the ferry-boat that sailed between Granton and Burntisland. I believe that Captain Morrison, whose Christian name I don't think I ever heard, was of Scandinavian origin. My mother, Nan, the Harrowers' second daughter, was very blonde, very Swedish-looking.

My father, Auld Willie's seventh child, was born in 1878 and his mother died when he was a baby. He was christened Frederick Burrows after my grandfather's greatest friend, an Englishman who had encouraged him in his love for music. My father, who was dark and slightly built but wiry, loved horses and wanted to be a jockey. But, like myself at a later time when I wanted to be an actor, he apparently did not know how to go about becoming one. Instead, thwarted, he became a groom, then a coachman, and then, in the progression or retrogression of civilisation – whichever way you look at it, and I prefer the second way – he became a chauffeur. He was a very good mechanic and kept all the cars he had in his care throughout the years in such perfect repair that his employers never had to pay garage bills. He passed on to me his love of horses but not his mechanical skill. I know nothing about machinery, and I don't want to know.

My parents married in 1909. My grandfather Harrower, an Elder of the Kirk and a non-drinker, got slightly tipsy at the wedding. This caused his eldest daughter, my Auntie Chrissie to say: "I'm black burning ashamed of you, Dad. It's bad enough you being Labour, but to be a tippler as well ... Oh dear, what will the minister say!" Auntie Chrissie was a great churchgoer and a great Tory. Although she had a good sense of ridicule and could be quite funny sometimes imitating her English neighbours in Dudley, the town in Worcestershire where she lived for most of her life, she was very straight-laced and her life was square-ruled by church. She was so shocked by my first novel that she hid the copy I'd sent her and would not allow my cousins, all grown men, to read it. They did, of course, in time, going to the public library and reading it surreptitiously.

When I was born on 12th July 1912 in a mews flat off Palmerston Place in Edinburgh, my father was chauffeur to wealthy, non-practising Dr Nasmyth, a director of the Fife Coal Company. I was only a few weeks old when I was taken to Duns in Berwickshire, where the Nasmyths had an estate. With the Nasmyths we moved from Duns to Torry House in Fifeshire soon after the outbreak of war in 1914. The first school I attended was in the village of Torryburn. The rest of my childhood was spent in moving from place to place. Whatever else I may have been, I was a well-travelled bairn in comparison with most bairns of that time.

In 1917 we went to Taymouth Castle in Perthshire when Dad became head chauffeur to the old Marquess of Breadalbane. The Breadalbane estate, one of the last great feudal properties in the United Kingdom, stretched from Aberfeldy to Argyllshire, and all over its hundreds of square miles the countrywomen curtseyed low whenever Auld Lordie or Lady B. drove by. My father was amused at first when he saw them apparently crouching with deferential heads in hedges and ditches as the Breadalbane limousine approached, but he soon got used to it.

Early in 1919 we returned to Edinburgh for a couple of years while Dad went touring all over Britain with rich Canadians. They wanted him to go to Canada with them, but he turned down their offer. Sometimes I wonder what my life might have been if I'd been brought up on their cattle ranch in Alberta. Instead, we went to Wigtownshire, to another chauffeuring job at Corsewall House outside the village of Kirkcolm on the shore of Loch Ryan.

This Wigtownshire estate belonging to the Carrick-Buchanans is the one I remember best. I spent four happy years there, going first to the village school, and then to

Stranraer High School. I still vividly recall going night after night with my mother, my two brothers and Mrs Henderson, the dairyman's wife, to the performances of a fifth-rate travelling theatre company, which stayed in Kirkcolm for 'a season' of about two months each year. They gave a different play each night in the village hall, and I saw many performances of *Uncle Tom's Cabin, Burke and Hare, The Face at the Window* and *The Murder in the Red Barn*. My mother and Mrs Henderson got very friendly with the actors and actresses, two or three families, who worked in the 'box office' and as ushers, as well as playing several roles in each play. And at the village school I sat next to a boy whose father played the parts of both Burke and Simon Legree, a generous man smelling of whisky, who occasionally treated me to a twopenny bar of Cadbury's milk chocolate or a whipped cream walnut in Mrs Hunter's wee shop. From this fit-up company and the occasional travelling film shows that had one-night-stands in the hall my love of the theatre and cinema was born.

Although we were poor, I don't consider that I had a deprived childhood. I was never hungry; I never went barefoot or existed on the legendary cold porridge; I always had nice clothes; we had a comfortable home; and for those days we had quite a lot of holidays, usually with my grandparents in Edinburgh or with aunties at Penicuik and Leven. My Grandfather Harrower used sometimes to say: "You're making a big mistake, ye ken, Nan, bringing these boys up like first-class passengers. They'll live to rue the day."

But Nan aye laughed and said: "Och away, Dad, I'm sure they'll manage."

My mother herself was a very good manager. She was a careful housewife, a good baker, and she made all her own jam and jelly, as well as keeping hens. She was not extravagant – except maybe about clothes. She loved clothes. She had a passion for hats, and as her youngest sister, Auntie Jess, was a

162

milliner, she was able to indulge this passion to the full. When she was an old woman – and she lived until she was eighty-four – she changed her dress twice or thrice a day, and every time she went out to the shops – and she did this oftener than she needed, I suspect, because she liked a gossip – she wore a different hat every time.

I get my spendthrift qualities from my father, who loved to buy things for us when we were children. Money just seemed to melt in his hands. He never drove his employers to Stranraer or any other town without bringing us back small gifts: copies of the *Boys' Own Paper* or the *Buffalo Bill Library* (which he loved to read himself!); sweets; spinning-tops of brightly striped metal; jigsaw puzzles; sticks of plasticine; propelling pencils; or toy pistols with rolls of 'caps' to make lovely bangs when we played Cowboys and Indians. We did not live near any other children; it was too far to go to the village for companionship, except when we were at school, so my brothers and I had to be content with each other. Bob and Morris were always the cowboys; I was always the Indian, the one who gets hunted. I made myself a feathered head-dress for this role: I sewed some hen feathers onto a red velvet band and wore it round my forehead. Daddy helped me make a tomahawk out of an old hammer and a piece of cardboard; he said, knowing me, that a tin axe-top would be too dangerous. And I made a wigwam out of birch branches in the wood behind our house, and I used to squat there for hours reading, after the other two had got tired of being cowboys and had gone on to something else. I was quite used to being the outsider in our boyhood games, it prepared me for life's bumps and grinds and somersaults.

Daddy made us a toboggan, but to our everlasting disappointment it snowed only once in the four winters we lived at Corsewall. Every year, though, he brought a small evergreen in from the wood and put it in a tub, and we had our Christmas tree, decorated with small coloured candles and shiny balls and strings of frosty tinsel, in times when it was not a widespread custom in Scotland to celebrate Christmas at all.

He put up a swing for us in the wood, too, and I used to swing there often, dreaming about what I'd do when we got the Urquhart Millions, building dream palaces overlooking the blue Mediterranean and log cabins in the wilds of Canada, until I swung myself into a daze and then gagged with nervous sickness and staggered off to vomit in the bushes – a truly dramatic performance that had no audience but the birds and squirrels.

My Grandfather Willie was fond of a dram. It was a failing he bequeathed to me, along with a fondness for young men in uniform. Unfortunately he did not bequeath any of his talent for playing musical instruments. Like millions of other youngsters in the 1920s, I tried to learn to play a ukelele, but I couldn't. I couldn't play a mouth organ; I couldn't even get a tune out of a paper and comb. But, among all my great ambitions – and I was teeming with all kinds of far-fetched dreams from being the lost heir to an Italian dukedom to bowing deeply to the applause in a great theatre in New York – one was to play the piano. It was not a very sensible ambition, I'm sure, but it gave me immense pleasure when a boy. It was something I believed would happen when the Urquhart Millions came. The Millions were not a myth but the key, the open sesame, to all manner of wondrous things. I would be like the young man in the advertisement. This advertisement, often seen in American film magazines like *Picture Play* and *Silver Screen*, bought out of Woolworths, concerned a shy diffident young man, who secretly took piano lessons by post and then, one night at a party, surprised everybody when he sat down at the piano. If I remember correctly, the punch line was: "Everybody laughed when I sat down to play, but they were struck dumb until they burst into spontaneous applause at the end of my performance." I truly believed that this would happen to me. Stardom as a second Paderewski was one of the many splendoured strands of my childhood pavilion.

When I was very small I often stayed with my Harrower grandparents for weeks on end. They loved to have me, for I was a delicate child, I did not play rough games, I did not like the company of other children, and I was cute enough to ape the manners and speech of the gentry. I used to kneel on a chair beside the kitchen table and watch Granny cooking, or I sat on the kitchen sofa beside Grandpa and read. I never had any wish to go outside, except when taken on a trip in a cable-car to the centre of Edinburgh.

My grandparents' cottage was full of fascinating objects. In the best room was a walnut whatnot crammed with a conglomeration of Victorian bric-à-brac, what an Angus friend calls a 'panjottery' of small glass and china ornaments. There were cups and saucers, milk jugs and plates with the armorial bearings and proud proclamations *A Present from Arbroath, A Wee Gift from Dunbar, A Memento of Burns Cottage, Alloway* and many others from John o' Groats to Berwick on Tweed. There was one of those painted wooden Russian dolls, a peasant woman, which unscrewed to reveal a smaller doll inside, and then another and another. There were fancy thimbles, trinket-boxes, all sorts of bright, often gaudy knick-knacks. In the best room, too, was a glass-doored cabinet with many shelves of books. I was allowed to take out one book at a time and read it while sitting beside Grandpa. So from the age of four I began, with some help, to read *Oliver Twist* and *East Lynne* and *Uncle Tom's Cabin.* I was also reading the serials in the *People's Friend* and the *Children's Newspaper,* which my grandmother bought specially for me. I would be seven or eight, I think, when I read "Emily of New Moon" in the *Children's Newspaper.* I was eight, I know, when I read the Tarzan books, and my life for a time was coloured by Jane and the jungle boy who (like me!) was really a lord, swinging from tree-top to tree-top to escape the perils of the jungle.

The object that fascinated me most at Granny's was the piano. It was a mahogany upright with two brass candlesticks sticking out above the keyboard. Although they always held bright red candles, these were never lit, as far as I can remember. The piano stood in the corner of the kitchen behind the sofa, which stretched from the fireside to the foot of the brass-railed double bed; the piano was thus completely closed in, and you had to step over the back of the sofa to get to it. Auntie Jess, the youngest, was the only member of the family who'd had piano lessons. She played with great verve, singing as she played. She could sing and play anything from *Riding Down To Bangor* to hymns, from *Smilin' Through* to popular Jazz. Jess was a pillar of Granton Parish Church choir, and she always sang in concerts. She was a member too of Mr Godfrey's Ladies Choir, a famous ensemble of that time. When I was quite small she was always taking me to the cinema, the zoo (which I hated), concerts and places of historical interest. She took me once to the gallery of the Usher Hall to hear a choral recital. I got such vertigo looking down from the upper tiers that I was sick and had to be hurried out. The same thing happened when she took me to the top of Sir Walter Scott's Monument. She was undaunted, however, and continued to take me to the cinema, even though, almost always, at the most exciting part of the film I had to be taken out to pee.

When she sang at home I always clambered over the sofa and stood beside her, watching her hands banging on the keys, and I used to join in the song and wish that I could play too. I couldn't sing, though. My mother and Granny always said: "You'll have to go outside to get the air, Freddie." They said plenty more, to drum it into me that, whatever other gifts I might have, singing wasn't amongst them.

But I persisted. As I've always persisted in whatever I've wanted to do. I am an ardent follower of Shakespeare's "perseverance keeps honour bright". There were two favourite songs I'd heard at the pierrots on the beach at Leven.

166

I stayed there for nearly the whole summer I was four with Auntie Bert and Uncle David, who had a pub; this was before they had any children of their own. Auntie Bert took me often to the pierrots' concerts, and I learnt the words of "Come With Me To Inverary" and "Memories".

When I went back to Edinburgh I sang "Come With Me To Inverary" to my grandparents, with abandon and actions copied from Ian, the dark attractive young pierrot tenor. Granny and Grandpa did not mind; I rather think they encouraged me. But Mrs McIntosh, an old Highland neighbour, who visited them every few days, did not relish my performance. She used to say: "That little poy shouldn't pe allowed to carry on like this. It is pad for the pairn, I am telling you, Mistress Harrower. It will pe spoiling him. He will grow up into a conceited young man."

The old Highland seer was right.

The other song, "Memories", is one I continued to sing and hum well beyond my childhood. I still sing sometimes in a cracked ginny voice, though I'm very careful now that nobody's within earshot:

> Childhood days, wild wood days
> Among the birds and bees.
> You left me alone,
> But still you're my own
> In my beautiful memories ...

I persisted in pursuit of piano-playing until I was maybe fourteen. Every time I went to my grandparents' home I fiddled about with the upright. They encouraged me; it was a diversion in their old age when they could not get about and had few visitors. I learned to read *sol fah* music, and I began to pick out tunes with one finger, then with one hand. As I got older I learned to 'vamp' with the other hand. I don't know what the neighbours thought (Mrs McIntosh was dead by then) but Granny was quite pleased. She and Grandpa used to sit and listen and, sometimes, sing as I 'played'. Their favourite and mine, which I could play from memory, was "Scots Wha' Hae". The neighbours must have been fervent patriots to be able to put up with it.

My attempted singing and playing were not, of course, important colours among the banners in my burnished pavilion. They had pastel or secondary hues. My brightest, my most glowing ambition until I was thirteen was to be an artist. I had drawn and painted ever since I was three or four and Mrs Nasmyth ('old Violet' as Ma used to call her) had given me a box of Reeves paints for Christmas. My schoolteachers considered me talented; I was always first at drawing in whatever school I went to. Floris Gillespie, the art teacher at Stranraer High School, where I was a pupil from 1924 to 1925, thought I might develop into a talented artist. She gave me every encouragement, and sent my drawings and paintings to the Dumfries and Galloway Fine Arts Society when it offered medals and diplomas for the best work submitted by pupils in the day schools of the three south-western Scottish counties. I did not win a medal, but I got a diploma and was highly commended for painting in the junior section. Flo Gillespie offered to take me to Dumfries, paying all expenses, to see the exhibition in the Assembly Rooms in April 1925, but I had to turn down her offer. Old Mr Carrick-Buchanan had just died, and we were preparing to leave Corsewall House. My father would have to get another job; the Urquharts would be on the wing again. A visit to an art exhibition had to give way to the hard facts of life.

While at Stranraer High School, where I spent the happiest year of my schooldays, I felt the first stirrings of the sexual impulses that have so gaily and excitingly coloured my splendoured pavilion for all the rest of my nights and days. In several classes I always sat next to Carmichael, a big good-looking boy, a farmer's son, who had enormous thighs encased in tight dark short trousers; for in those days boys didn't start to wear 'longs' until they were at least fourteen. I inspected his thighs with pleasure every time I sat close to him. His backside was the first male one I ever gazed at with admiration and lust, though I didn't know the meaning of that last word then. I've always regretted I never laid a hand on it. I was greatly enamoured of Carmichael. (This is not his real name.) I was enamoured too of one of the masters, Mr Maycock, a handsome broad-shouldered young man with smooth dark hair. I was one of Mr Maycock's favourites because I was always near the top of the class in the subject he taught. But Mr Maycock was not enamoured of Carmichael; nor was Carmichael of him. Carmichael was not a dullard, yet somehow or other he always aroused Mr Maycock's wrath. Whenever Carmichael made a mistake Mr Maycock would open his desk, take out the rolled-up tawse and throw it at Carmichael, ordering him to bring it to the front of the class. If Carmichael was slow to comply, Mr Maycock, a hefty rugger-player, would spring at him and haul him from his seat by the scruff of the neck. Then he would belt him, giving him far more than the offence merited. He could not hide his delight in belting him. When Carmichael was allowed to return to the seat beside me, trying to keep back the snivels and pressing his hurt hands between his thighs, I used to nearly faint with terror and excitement.

I don't think I ever thought of myself as another Reynolds or Stubbs (I was always drawing women's heads and horses) but I did fancy myself as a dress-designer. I was madly interested in women's clothes. In those days Bessie Ascough was a regular contributor to the *Daily Mail*, which we got all the time we were at Corsewall. I studied her drawings and copied them, and they gave me ideas for my own designs. I often drew, too, scenes for stage plays, for I built myself a toy theatre out of thick cardboard. But this desire to express myself by drawing and painting dwindled after my thirteenth birthday. It gave way to the greater ambitions to be an author and an actor. It did not die all at once, of course; it floundered like someone in a swamp, and then, more or less, gave up the ghost. It has never really died. Even yet, in my old age, there are moments when, to amuse myself or a child, I will draw horses or women's heads.

While I was at Kirkcolm Village School we had, for a couple of years, a schoolmaster of literary bent. He had lived for a long time in Australia, and he was a great one for giving us odd subjects for essays. Sometimes he would ask us to try and write a story rather than an essay. I wrote several 'adventure' stories for him; they were inspired by reading *Coral Island* and *Martin Rattler* and Captain Mayne-Reid's *The Last of the Incas* (or was it called *Montezuma's Daughter?*), all of them borrowed from the library in the Big House. Mr Carrick-Buchanan, who was on the verge of ninety, liked the little Urquhart boys to visit him, and he always encouraged us to return by lending us books from his library.

The Australian liked my stories, and he read them aloud to the pupils in the Big End, the four senior classes in the two-roomed school, as opposed to the infants in the Wee End. One of the essays he read aloud was about what I'd do if I were a great film star. Heartened by this, I wrote a fairy story and sent it (accompanied by a drawing) to the *Weekly Scotsman*. The story was printed in the Children's Column, edited by 'Greatheart', in either 1924 or 1925. It was my first appearance in print.

My love affair with the cinema – the most dazzling colour (apart from sex) in the pavilion of my youth – started after we left Wigtownshire and went back to Edinburgh, where my father got a job with a whisky firm, which lasted until he retired. Up to that time I had, of course, seen only occasional films; I remember Auntie Jess taking me to see Mary Pickford in *Daddy Long Legs*. I remember it best, because I was haunted for years by the scene in which the wicked housekeeper or the wicked orphanage superintendent (I have no idea which)

170

seized little Mary's finger and pressed it on the hot grate as a punishment for something or other. But I did not become a real film fan, or 'buff' as they're called now, until we settled in Edinburgh for good.

Those were the days of the twopenny matinées. Actually, there were three prices: a penny for the front seats, twopence for the stalls, and threepence for the balcony. Bob and Morris and I went every Saturday afternoon to the twopenny seats in either the Grand or the Savoy in Stockbridge or the Salon in Leith Walk. There were several picture houses our mother didn't approve of us visiting in case we came home with unwelcome creepy-crawlies as close companions; so we usually rang the changes on the same three. I can remember Saturdays when we went to a twopenny matinée and then to another cinema, where we could get into the cheapest seats for fourpence, at night. Apart from Saturdays, I always managed to go once or twice to the pictures during the week.

I still have a small metal-covered notebook with a crest and *British Empire Exhibition, Wembley 1925* on its front. It was given me by one of Jess's young men who, greatly daring, had made the adventurous trip to London and the Exhibition. In this notebook I recorded all the films I saw then. Here are some entries: Nita Naldi, Leatrice Joy, Estelle Taylor, Richard Dix and Rod La Rocque in *The Ten Commandments* on 2nd September 1925; Marie Prevost, Monte Blue and Helene Chadwick in *The Dark Swan*, 23rd September 1925; Norma Talmadge in *The Isle of Conquest*, 3rd October 1925; Norma Shearer and Conrad Nagel in *Excuse Me*, 3rd October 1925; Corinne Griffith in *Love's Wilderness*, 10th October 1925; Douglas Fairbanks in *The Thief of Bagdhad*, 6th October 1925; and Rod La Rocque and Jacqueline Logan in *Code of the Sea*, 7th October 1925.

Gloria Swanson and Pola Negri were my favourite stars. I never missed their films. The first time I saw Pola Negri, she was starring in *Men*. The first Swanson film was *The Humming Bird*. In this Gloria was a *gamin* of the Paris gutters, dressed in boy's clothes à la Jackie Coogan in *The Kid* (with Charlie Chaplin). Then I saw her in *Manhandled*. Here she was a little New York shopgirl who masqueraded in one scene as an exiled Russian countess in order to attract customers into the store. She sat at a samovar and dispensed tea. A large society dame rushed up to her and broke into voluble Russian. Gloria did not know what to do, so she took refuge in tears. The leading man (I think he was Ian Keith, a male star of the period) had to explain to the lady that the Countess was too overcome at hearing her native tongue to be able to reply.

Of such stuff was my long cinematic amour made! But I didn't think it did me any harm. It was healthier than getting high on marijuana or LSD.

Other favourite stars were Norma Talmadge, Betty Compson, Betty Blythe, Florence Vidor, Thomas Meighan, Lon Chaney, Adolphe Menjou, Alice Terry, Ramon Novarro, Valentino ... the list is endless. And, of course, there were Tom Mix, Buck Jones, Ken Maynard and Hoot Gibson, the cowboy heroes of the time. I loved cowboys, and still do.

As I got older, besides going to the cinema two and three times a week, I went also once a week to the gallery of either the King's Theatre or the Royal Lyceum. I think the first play I ever saw was *Peter Pan*. I was seven or eight, and was taken to it by Auntie Jess. I remember standing in the queue for the gallery of the old Theatre Royal, on that steep incline overlooking the top of Leith Walk. It was to the Theatre Royal, too, that Jess took me and my brothers to see several pantomimes. I see in the *Wembley* notebook that I saw *Goldilocks and the Three Bears* on 2nd February 1926. I don't remember anything about it, though I do remember another panto where everybody, chorus and principals, were dressed as Christmas crackers. It was at the Theatre Royal that I often saw and laughed so much at that wonderful female impersonator, Tommy Lorne. I loved the old Theatre Royal, and I regret that it is no more. I regret, too, that it was not on its stage but the stage of the Royal Lyceum that I made my one and only appearance as an extra in *Back to Methuselah*.

When I was seventeen or eighteen, by that time almost desperate to go on the stage or films but not knowing how to go about achieving it, I was going weekly to see the Macdona Players in a repertory season at the Lyceum. Esmé Percy was the leading actor and director. I took the plunge and wrote to him, saying I wanted to be an actor. He sent me a card inviting me to go and see him. The result was that, with a number of other Edinburgh teenagers, I 'walked on' in the last great act of Shaw's play. Clad in a Greek tunic, with my bare arms and legs smeared with milk-coffee-coloured slap, I stood at the back of the stage, clutching a spear in my tiny frozen hand, for hours and hours for two nights while the Ancients made their long declamations. I never made another attempt to go on the stage, though the experience did not dampen my stage and film ambitions. It made me concentrate more and more, however, on my other ambition to be a writer; I thought that maybe if I got a book published I'd become famous and then it would be easier to get on the stage.

I won a bursary of ten pounds a year to enable me to go to Stranraer High School. Through the good offices of Dr Thomas Nasmyth, whom we visited every now and then, the last two years of this bursary were transferred to Broughton Secondary School in Edinburgh. I went reluctantly to Broughton and loathed it. I was thankful to leave in the summer I was fifteen. I had no inclination for further schooling. I got a job in a bookshop near the university at a wage of ten shillings a week.

I worked in this shop for seven years. And all that time I dreamed of being somewhere else. In the long hours between eight-thirty in the morning to seven o'clock (and often later) at night, in the long intervals between customers, when I wasn't dusting old theological and medical books and making price tickets, I read an enormous amount: everything that appealed to me from Gibbon's *Decline and Fall of the Roman Empire* to

Knut Hamsun's *Growth of the Soil* and Flaubert's *Salambo*, from Edgar Wallace to Oliver Sandys, P.G. Wodehouse and Galsworthy. It was, I like to think, a better grounding for a writer than any university. Although I hated the long hours, the monotony and the poor pay, I suppose those years in the bookshop helped to develop me as a writer; the customers certainly taught me a lot about human nature and they made me even more ambitious, spurring me on to try to escape from them to a richer, fuller and pleasanter life.

And so, hidden in a corner behind the counter and at nights when I went home and at week-ends, I wrote three novels and a lot of short stories. I sent the novels – in longhand, since I had no typewriter – to countless publishers. My poor mother got used to seeing the postman bring them back with great regularity. I got used to it, too. Every rejection just made me go on writing with greater fury. None of those novels ever got published, of course. The manuscripts of the first two are in the vaults of the National Library of Scotland in Edinburgh. The MS of the third will, I hope, join them after I've used some material in it for a work in progress.

My fourth novel, written after I'd left the bookshop, was the first to find a publisher. This was *Time Will Knit*. It was published a year before the outbreak of the Second World War, which so effectively muddied and tattered and destroyed so many of the gorgeous colours and splendours of not only mine but many other youthful pavilions.

SELECTED BIBLIOGRAPHY

Time will Knit (1938); *The Clouds are Big with Mercy* (1946); *The Ferret was Abraham's Daughter* (1949); *Jezebel's Dust* (1951); *The Dying Stallion* (1967); *The Ploughing Match* (1968).